Empath and Narcissist

Stop The Cycle of Toxic Relationships, Heal From Narcissistic Abuse, and Thrive as a Sensitive Person

Rachel West

Table of Content

Introduction

I magine yourself sitting in a crowded room feeling very lonely. Even when everyone around you is having a great time, all you can pick up on is the subtle undertone of emotions; anxiety covered up by laughter, agony concealed behind smiles. You feel exhausted and take in these feelings as though they were your own, yet you are unable to turn them off. The life of an empath is one in which they are profoundly rooted in the emotional realm, yet frequently encounter difficulties in establishing their own identity and emotional equilibrium. Now picture that there is another person in the same room. They effortlessly entice others to them with their charisma and self-assurance. However, their seeming interest in people is only superficial; their friendly exterior belies a deeper incapacity to establish sincere emotional bonds. This is the world of the narcissist, who is essentially cut off from genuine empathy but thrives on praise and attention. The difference between narcissists and empaths is not merely the story of two different personalities; it is a dynamic that manifests itself in families, relationships, and workplaces and frequently leaves an emotional trail of chaos in its aftermath.

You may find yourself in this familiar situation: lured into relationships that seem intense and promising at first, only to wind up exhausted, misinterpreted, or controlled. Giving without end, you experience other people's feelings as though they were your own, frequently at the price of your well-being. In a world that often takes too much, empaths are givers. These experiences are not merely personal struggles; rather, they point to a larger problem with our comprehension and management of emotional connections. The dance between empathy and self-preservation, or understanding others and understanding oneself, is where the problem lies. Many people find themselves in this dance, frequently without even understanding the moves they are performing or the reasons behind them.

The issue for empaths is a persistent emotional overload that causes them to feel overwhelmed by other people's feelings. This can result in exhaustion, worry, and a loss of identity. Narcissists' incapacity to truly connect with their feelings results in flimsy relationships and a pervasive sense of discontent. Individual personalities are only one aspect of this dynamic; the other is how these personalities interact, frequently in destructive and unsustainable ways. It is a loop of comprehension and misinterpretation, attraction and repulsion, need and disregard. Many people find themselves caught in this loop, with no idea how to escape or alter the pattern. It is critical at this pivotal point to comprehend the relationships between empathy and self-preservation. It is about going deeper than meets the eye and learning how these characteristics combine to shape your life. A stronger sense of self-awareness provides you with the knowledge and skills necessary to negotiate challenging emotional terrain on the path to equilibrium and well-being.

Establishing boundaries, understanding emotional limits, and developing a strong sense of self in the face of other people's emotions are all part of the journey for those who identify as empaths. It is important to turn empathic abilities from a potential source of fatigue into a source of strength. This is a difficult process that calls for honesty and fortitude to change ingrained thought and behavior habits. However, there are substantial benefits as well, such as happier relationships, a more profound sense of self, and a full existence. The next steps involve integrating this knowledge now that you are aware of these dynamics. Positive change can be cultivated in your life and relationships by accepting and putting into practice ideas and tactics that resonate with you.

Digging into the pages of this book is akin to unlocking a door to a more profound understanding of yourself as well as the complex dynamics of interpersonal relationships. It delves further beyond the basic classifications of narcissists and empaths, exploring the essence of what it means to connect, feel, and understand on a profound level. Imagine learning things that shed light on how intricate your emotional world is. This book provides a journey of self-discovery, regardless of whether you find yourself greatly impacted by the emotions of those around you or find it difficult to comprehend and articulate your feelings. It involves unraveling the layers of your emotional experiences to see how they affect the way you communicate and engage with others. It gives you insight into controlling the level of your emotional empathy. It is about discovering methods to accept your sensitivity without sacrificing your emotional stability. It is a quest to accept your innate ability to empathize as a part of who you are. You will discover perspectives and methods that can change the way you interact with people, resulting in more fulfilling and harmonious relationships. It involves developing empathy and respect for one another by learning to navigate the emotional terrain of both you and the people you contact with.

This book is a collection of personal reflections, insights, and experiences that resonate with the challenges and joys of being empathic or understanding narcissistic traits. It is a story that connects the dots between emotional understanding, providing a rich and insightful knowledge tapestry. However, it is more than just a compilation of facts; it is a companion in your journey toward emotional understanding and relationship growth. It is an exploration of the depths of human emotions and the beauty of understanding them. Navigating our own and others' emotional currents is not just helpful, but crucial in a world where relationships mold our everyday experiences. Since there are new interactions and challenges every day, we must comprehend these dynamics right away. This book contains techniques and ideas that have the power to significantly improve your relationships, self-awareness, and quality of life.

Today's world moves quickly, and our means of connection and communication are always changing. The ability to control and comprehend one's emotions is vital in this constantly shifting environment. Every interaction offers a possibility for development and a closer bond since there is always a chance to put these principles into practice. If this path of self-discovery is postponed, everyday chances for growth and happier connections will be lost. Every conversation and every obstacle presents an opportunity for practice and the application of the knowledge you will gain. As soon as you begin using this wisdom, your life will start to transform. This goes beyond merely gathering information; it involves actively participating in a process of growth and understanding. It is a dedication to improving your emotional intelligence and strengthening your bonds.

Choosing to embark on this journey is a step toward improving your relationships and regaining control over your emotional health. Every step taken on the path to deeper emotional knowledge and connection is a step closer to leading a wiser and more compassionate life. Now is the perfect time to get started since every second presents a chance for development and a deeper connection.

Before the insights and perspectives provided in this book, navigating the emotional terrain of narcissist and empath relations was frequently a confusing and misunderstood journey. Many become mired in relationships or personal conflicts without knowing why they are feeling so helpless or disengaged. The way to better relationships and emotional clarity appeared unattainable, like a puzzle with missing pieces.

Without the means to safeguard their emotional health, empaths found it difficult to control the torrent of intense feelings from people around them. They frequently struggled to discern between their own emotions and those of others, feeling as though they were lost in a sea of emotions. Life was a tiring roller coaster of highs and lows in terms of emotions until they learned how to moderate their empathic powers and set boundaries. Many were forced to manage their relationships and emotional environment by trial and error in the lack of explicit, helpful direction. Healthy relationships and emotional understanding were frequently the result of a lengthier, more difficult path fraught with uncertainty and mistakes.

With the information and strategies in this book at your disposal, you can approach the situation from a new angle and fill in the missing pieces of the puzzle. They provide a clearer path to understanding and navigating these complex emotional dynamics. With this newfound knowledge, the journey that once seemed difficult and full of obstacles becomes more accessible and empowering. There is a feeling of familiarity that connects with your experiences as you turn the pages of this book. It feels as though the lines were written with an understanding of the emotional trips, difficulties, and questions you have encountered. This book gives you ideas that seem to speak directly to your quest for a deeper understanding.

This book will be a helpful ally if you have ever felt overpowered by the intensity of your own emotions or the emotions of people around you, or if you have had difficulty forging genuine connections. It tackles these situations with an uncommon depth and understanding. It is intended for people who have successfully negotiated the challenges of having a high degree of empathy or who have struggled with the nuances of their emotional terrain. You will discover true-to-life tales and scenarios within its pages, as well as practical guidance and introspective observations that resonate with your innermost thoughts. This book provides useful advice on navigating the emotional world with grace and courage while acknowledging the subtleties of being fully connected to it.

This is a journey of validation and discovery, not just something to read. You will feel enlightened after reading each chapter, knowing that your individual experiences are acknowledged and understood. You will find yourself going back to this guide again and again, taking away new perspectives and affirmations with each reading. In this book, you will find a companion for your journey toward greater self-awareness and enriched relationships. It is a resource that speaks to your needs, challenges, and aspirations, guiding you toward a path of emotional empowerment and deeper connections.

Chapter 1:
Identifying Empaths and Narcissists

The Traits and Characteristics of an Empath

I magine being able to sense everyone's mood the moment you walk into a room. While this may seem like a superpower to others, empaths have to deal with it daily. People who are extremely sensitive to the feelings and energies of others are known as empaths. They do not just sympathize; they experience other people's feelings as though they were their own. This profound empathy has its benefits and drawbacks.

The life of an empath is like a sponge, soaking in all the emotions and energies in their environment. Because of their increased sensitivity, empaths frequently need to withdraw, to recharge and restore their emotional balance. It is not just about feeling sad when someone else is sad; it is about experiencing that sadness deeply, often without the need for words or explanations. It is common to describe empaths as having overly sensitive hearts. This is a lived reality, not just poetic language. They are the family members who always seem to know when something is wrong, the pals who will cry with you, and the coworkers who pick up on your unsaid stress. Their uncommon capacity for profound interpersonal connection makes them indispensable in fields like education, counseling, and medical care. However, being an empath is not just about emotions. It is about a deeper understanding of the human condition. Sensing things beneath the surface, empaths frequently possess a keen sense of intuition. A small shift in someone's tone or body language, for example, could be picked up on by them that others could miss. Although intuitive knowledge can be an effective instrument, it can also be overpowering, particularly in situations where there are several stimuli present. Also, empaths frequently have a very imaginative and creative mind. In the arts, whether it be acting, writing, painting, or music, they often find comfort. These pursuits provide a channel for their deep feelings and a means of expressing the strong emotions they harbor.

But there are difficulties with being an empath. Excessive emotional input can cause physical symptoms like weariness and anxiety. Because their innate desire is to assist and heal, empaths frequently find it difficult to set limits. They could end up in relationships where the giving takes precedence over receiving in terms of their own emotional needs. Emotional overload is another danger that empaths must avoid. They have to learn how to safeguard their fragile souls in a cruel and intimidating environment. This could be as simple as taking time to unwind in nature, learning to say "no," or engaging in self-care.

Empaths serve as a reminder of the significance of connection and vulnerability in a world that frequently prizes stoicism and strength. They demonstrate to us that having strong feelings is a great strength rather than a weakness. Understanding the empath teaches us not only about them but about human emotion in all its complexities and depth. The fact that empaths are gifted with sensitivity should be kept in mind as we learn more about their world. It permits an exquisite and uncommon degree of comprehension and empathy. As mirrors of our emotional reality, empaths reflect the richness of our shared humanity and are more than merely feeling beings.

The Traits and Characteristics of a Narcissist

The narcissist stands in sharp contrast to the world of profound emotional connection inhabited by empaths. Imagine someone entering the same room as everyone else, but instead of feeling the emotions of others around them, their main concerns are on how they would be seen and what they stand to gain from the interactions. This is the world of the narcissist, a personality type distinguished by an exaggerated perception of one's significance, an intense desire for excessive attention and admiration, and a lack of empathy toward others. Many times, narcissism is misinterpreted. It is a more intricate and frequently harmful pattern of behavior than simply being conceited or overconfident. Narcissism stems from a weak sense of self that is easily damaged by small setbacks. Because of this, narcissists tend to shun challenging individuals and instead associate with those who bolster their ego.

A sense of entitlement is a major characteristic of narcissists. They think they are unique and should be treated as such. There are several ways this can show up, such as feeling entitled to special treatment and expecting unceasing praise. They frequently have an inflated sense of self and may overestimate their abilities and accomplishments. They may also fantasize about having limitless wealth, power, intelligence, beauty, or the perfect partner. People find themselves drawn to charming and charismatic narcissists. They can captivate people by presenting positive narratives and using their charm to exert control and influence. But this attractiveness can easily give way to haughtiness and conceit, particularly when their sense of dominance is challenged.

Dealing with a narcissist can be extremely challenging because of their lack of empathy. They find it difficult to identify and address the needs and emotions of other people. This is not to say that they cannot sense other people's emotions; rather, it just means that they usually do not care about other people's feelings unless it benefits them. Because they view other people as objects to be utilized to satisfy their own goals and desires, narcissists frequently engage in manipulative or exploitative behavior. They might use other people for their benefit, not caring how their actions affect those around them.

Relationships with narcissists might be especially difficult. They frequently entail an idealization and devaluation cycle. During the idealization stage, the narcissist shows their partner a lot of love and attention, but later on, they devalue them by showing disdain, criticism, and emotional disengagement. People caught in this loop may experience confusion, pain, and a feeling of having to walk on eggshells around the narcissist.

Knowing that narcissism is a spectrum disorder is crucial. The degree to which these characteristics are present varies widely, and not all narcissists are the same. Some narcissists are more aggressive and paranoid, and more likely to take advantage of others, while others may show more subdued symptoms. Understanding narcissism is essential for society at large as well as for individuals who deal with narcissists. It aids in our understanding of the warning signals of unhealthy relationships as well as the value of empathy and genuine connection. We discover the intricacies of the human ego and the ramifications of a life devoid of empathy while exploring the narcissist's world.

Why Empaths and Narcissists Are Attracted to Each Other

Though narcissists lack empathy and have a great need for admiration, it may seem strange that empaths, who are known for their profound sense of compassion and empathy, are drawn to them. This attraction, however, is not only widespread but also complicated, involving a unique interplay of psychological dynamics. This attraction is driven by a strong, though frequently unconscious, dynamic. Empaths, with their natural ability to sense and absorb the emotions of others, are drawn to the pain and vulnerability that often lie hidden beneath the narcissist's facade of confidence and grandiosity. They see the wounded soul behind the mask and are compelled to help, heal, and understand. Since empaths are natural nurturers, they find someone in a narcissist who appears to need their support and understanding.

The empath is the ultimate source of validation and attention for the narcissist. They need empathy and attention, and empaths provide it to them—often without asking anything in return. For the narcissist, this produces an ideal situation in which they can get the support and emotional labor they require without having to provide anything in return. For both parties, this relationship can feel incredibly fulfilling at first. The need to help and establish a strong relationship with another person is satisfied when the empath feels appreciated and needed. The narcissist feels admired and understood and relishes the emotional support and undivided attention.

But this dynamic can turn toxic very rapidly. Giving more and more may become a habit for the empath as they attempt to satisfy the narcissist's never-ending emotional needs. In the process, they could begin to forget themselves and continuously put the narcissist's wants ahead of their own. Because of their intense empathy and unwillingness to give up on people, empaths are prone to continuing in emotionally draining and unsatisfying relationships. But, the narcissist may begin to reveal their genuine selves after initially putting on a front of charm and affection. As the empath keeps giving, the narcissist could start to take it for granted and start to expect constant support without giving anything back. As a result of feeling increasingly devalued and unloved, the empath may perceive the relationship as a one-way street.

The desire to change the narcissist is another factor driving this attraction for the empath. Maybe they think that if they give the narcissist enough love and compassion, they will see their destructive actions and change. Regretfully, as narcissism is an ingrained personality trait that is difficult to modify, this is rarely the case. An intricate ballet of psychological patterns and emotional needs drives the attraction between narcissists and empaths. It is a dynamic that can be challenging to disrupt, frequently needing the empath to acknowledge their value and the significance of establishing boundaries. Learning that no amount of empathy can alter someone unwilling to change themselves is a painful lesson.

Both narcissists and empaths need to understand this dynamic. Empaths must understand their worth and the necessity of taking care of themselves. For narcissists, it is about realizing how their actions affect other people and how important empathy and respect for one another are in relationships.

The Complex Intersection of the Dark Empath

The concept of the "dark empath" presents an intriguing and nuanced character in the narrative of empathy and narcissism. Dark empaths are individuals who have the intuitive and sensitive traits of empaths together with other behaviors more commonly associated with narcissism. This intersection creates a unique personality type that contradicts the traditional understanding that empathy and narcissism are mutually exclusive.

Similar to traditional empaths, dark empaths are sensitive to other people's emotions and feelings. They can perceive and understand the feelings of those around them. They might, however, exploit this knowledge for their benefit, in contrast to traditional empaths. They have a certain amount of emotional intelligence, but they might also decide to combine self-serving behaviors with emotional manipulation or exploitation of others. Because of this duality, dark empaths can be especially difficult to recognize and understand. On the surface, they may appear compassionate and understanding, often using their empathic abilities to build trust and rapport. But like a narcissist, their objectives may be driven by a desire for control, admiration, or validation.

Because of their ability to understand and manipulate emotions, dark empaths are often quite successful in social situations. They are generally charismatic and engaging, able to adapt their behavior to suit different people and contexts. This adaptability, however, can also lead to a lack of authenticity in their interactions and relationships. Dealing with dark empaths can be difficult because of their ability to blend in and hide their manipulative tendencies. They may not exhibit the overt grandiosity or entitlement typical of narcissists, making their behavior subtler and harder to detect. They can be charming and likable, using their empathic skills to create a facade of genuineness and concern. Dark empaths can be particularly confusing in relationships. They may exhibit moments of genuine care and understanding, interspersed with manipulative and self-centered behaviors. This inconsistency can leave partners feeling uncertain and destabilized, unsure of the true nature of the dark empath's feelings and intentions.

It is critical to understand the concept of the dark empath for several reasons. It disproves the idea that empaths and narcissists are mutually exclusive and shows that these traits can coexist in complex ways. It also emphasizes the importance of intention behind empathic behavior. True empathy involves not only understanding others' emotions but also caring about their well-being selflessly. Self-awareness is crucial for people who relate to dark empath characteristics. Aiming for authenticity and genuine connections while acknowledging the possibility of manipulation can promote healthier relationships and personal growth. Setting boundaries and being aware is essential for anyone dealing with dark empaths to prevent manipulation or harm.

The dark empath represents a nuanced view of human behavior, where empathy and narcissism intersect in unexpected ways. It serves as a reminder that understanding human emotions and motivations is a complex endeavor that calls for a thorough exploration of the various nuances of empathy.

Recognizing the Hidden Manipulation of Covert Narcissists

The subtler, more pernicious kind of narcissism is displayed by the covert narcissist, who is often less talked about than their overt counterpart. The characteristics of a covert narcissist are harder to identify and understand since they are less obvious than those of an overt narcissist, who exhibits grandiosity and attention-seeking behaviors. Relationships and interactions may be significantly impacted by this covert manipulation. Many characteristics of overt narcissists, such as a lack of empathy and a desire for admiration, are also present in covert narcissists, although these characteristics are sometimes concealed under a front of sensitivity or humility. They might not demand attention or publicly brag about their accomplishments. Rather, their narcissism manifests itself in subtler and indirect ways.

One of the main traits of covert narcissists is their tendency to play the victim. They often give the impression that they are misunderstood, unappreciated, or mistreated. By adopting a victim mindset, they can get sympathy and attention, while also justifying their negative behaviors. They may use guilt or pity to manipulate others into providing the attention and validation they crave. Covert narcissists can be passive-aggressive in their communication style. Through sarcasm, silent treatment, or backhanded compliments, they can subtly convey their annoyance or rage. This indirect expression of hostility can be confusing and hurtful to those around them, leaving them unsure of where they stand. Sensitivity to criticism is another characteristic shared by covert narcissists. They may not react to perceived slights or criticism with the overt rage of an overt narcissist, but they are nonetheless deeply impacted. They may react with withdrawal, sulking, or subtle retaliation. Their narcissistic behaviors are an attempt to cover up their underlying insecurities and low self-esteem, which often cause them to be overly sensitive.

Covert narcissists can be emotionally draining in relationships. They might provide little in return and need constant reassurance and attention. It may be challenging for them to truly care for their partners' needs and feelings due to their lack of empathy. Additionally, they could be easily jealous, seeing their partner's success or independence as a threat to their self-esteem.

Understanding subtle manipulative behaviors is essential to identifying a covert narcissist. It is critical to recognize behaviors that involve victimization, passive-aggressiveness, and sensitivity to criticism. Setting boundaries and taking care of oneself is essential for people who are dealing with covert narcissists. Avoiding being sucked into their manipulative dynamics can be made easier by being aware of these patterns. It is critical to understand that the actions of the covert narcissist are an expression of their own needs and fears rather than a reflection of your worth. When navigating these challenging relationships, it can be helpful to ask friends, family, or professionals for support.

The covert narcissist serves as a reminder that narcissism is not always loud and obvious. It can be hidden behind a mask of vulnerability, requiring a deeper level of awareness and understanding to recognize and address.

Chapter 2:
The Empath's Vulnerability to Narcissists

The Unique Vulnerability of a Sigma Empath

I magine an observer with a sharp and discerning eye standing quietly on the periphery of a social gathering. This person, who might seem detached or aloof at first glance, is what we call a "sigma empath." With their distinct route, sigma empaths differ from the more commonly known alpha or beta personalities. Their preference for solitude or a close-knit group of people over huge social gatherings illustrates their independence and self-sufficiency. Oddly enough, though, narcissists may find them an unexpected target because of these same qualities.

The sigma empath is an intriguing study in contrasts. Despite their great empathy and ability to feel other people's emotions, they often decide to avoid getting involved in emotional situations. Their independence is not a sign of coldness, but rather a self-defense mechanism, a way to manage the overwhelming input of the emotional world around them. That independence, however, might serve as a beacon to attract narcissists. Since narcissists enjoy a challenge and the rush of taking down someone's walls, the sigma empath's independence offers just that. The narcissist sees in the sigma empath a fortress to conquer; a validation of their ability to affect even the most independent person.

The initial approaches made by a narcissist can be perplexing to a sigma empath. At first, they could reject the advances as they are accustomed to being independent. But the narcissist's charm and apparent interest can be seductive, especially if it feels like an acknowledgment of the sigma empath's often-overlooked qualities. The narcissist, skilled in manipulation, may play a game of cat and mouse, drawing the sigma empath in with attention and admiration, then pulling away, creating a push-pull dynamic that can be both confusing and compelling. In this dynamic, the sigma empath's innate tendency to understand and heal might turn into a weakness. They might interpret the narcissist's actions as a cry for help or a sign of hidden pain, that they alone can relieve. This may cause them to fall into a trap where they use all of their energy to attempt to "fix" the narcissist, resulting in a fundamentally imbalanced relationship.

The superficiality and self-centeredness of the narcissist are fundamentality at odds with the authenticity and depth that the sigma empath values in relationships. However, the narcissist's ability to mirror and mimic emotional depth can temporarily deceive even the most discerning empath. The sigma empath could be tempted into a relationship that seems to offer depth and understanding but in fact, leads to emotional anguish and manipulation. Recognizing this vulnerability is essential for sigma empaths. It entails realizing their worth and the significance of their independence, not just as a shield, but as a source of strength. It also entails realizing that, although empathy is a gift, others who do not care for them can take advantage of it.

In the intricate relationship dynamic between the sigma empath and the narcissist, understanding the difference between manipulative mirroring and genuine emotional depth is crucial for the sigma empath. To ensure that their empathic nature is involved in healthy, reciprocal relationships rather than one-sided emotional exploits, this discernment is essential in managing these interactions.

Why Narcissists Prey on Empaths

Due to their innate ability to see and understand the feelings of others, empaths are frequently targeted by narcissists. This section explores why narcissists, who are skilled at taking advantage of the generosity and giving nature of empaths for their gain, find these people appealing.

Empaths are givers by nature. They possess an innate ability to listen, understand, and offer compassion. This propensity to prioritize the needs of others over one's own can become a double-edged sword. When a narcissist is around, this selfless trait can be perverted into a tool for manipulation. Narcissists, who often lack genuine empathy, find in empaths a source of unending attention and emotional support—resources they yearn for but are unable to give back. Because of their innate desire to heal and help, empaths may unintentionally fall victim to a narcissist's trap. Empaths frequently aim to form deep, meaningful connections when they enter relationships. Narcissists, recognizing this desire, may present a facade of being open, vulnerable, and in need of help. To an empath, this perceived vulnerability is a call to action—an opportunity to provide care and support. But this dynamic can easily go out of balance. The empath may begin to invest an increasing amount of their emotional energy in the relationship out of a desire to be helpful and supportive. Conversely, the narcissist absorbs this energy and provides little to nothing in return. The empath may feel emotionally exhausted, drained, and unappreciated as a result of this imbalance.

Another factor that makes empaths attractive to narcissists is their tolerance for highly emotional situations. Empaths are often willing to work through emotional pain and conflict, qualities that narcissists exploit to create a sense of drama and urgency in the relationship. This can result in a vicious cycle where the narcissist keeps pushing boundaries and creating chaos while the empath feels responsible for maintaining the relationship's emotional well-being. Additionally, empaths tend to be forgiving and understanding—qualities that narcissists may exploit to justify their harmful behavior. The empath's willingness to see the good in others and give second chances can be twisted by the narcissist into an opportunity to continue their manipulative behaviors without consequence.

Empaths must identify these tendencies and understand why they may be particularly vulnerable to narcissistic people. Although their compassion and empathy are strong and admirable qualities, they need to be balanced with awareness and self-protection. In addition to realizing that it is not their responsibility to mend or heal everyone they come into contact with, empaths must learn to spot the telltale indications of emotional exploitation and manipulation.

Consider the case of Anna, a classic empath, who met David, a charismatic man with narcissistic tendencies, at a volunteer event in the neighborhood. Anna was immediately drawn to David's charm and his seemingly vulnerable stories about his struggles in life. Her empathic nature kicked in, and she found herself offering support and understanding. As their relationship progressed, Anna found herself increasingly invested in David's well-being. She would spend hours listening to his problems, offering advice, and supporting him emotionally. David, on the other hand, played the role of the victim perfectly, always emphasizing his need for Anna's unique understanding and support. However, Anna soon began to notice that the relationship was taking a toll on her. She was constantly drained, often putting her own needs and emotions last. Every time she tried to address this imbalance, David would skillfully turn the conversation around, pointing out how he was the one in need and how she was the only one who could help him.

You can learn from Anna and David's experience how critical it is to always be mindful of how your kind gestures are perceived and returned. The unbalanced nature of their relationship serves as a sharp reminder that, although empathy is a commendable quality, it should not result in emotional exhaustion or self-neglect. This situation also emphasizes how important it is that you be able to spot tiny indicators of manipulation. In your sincere attempts to help, you may fail to see or justify behaviors that are, in reality, exploitative. It is important to be nice and understanding, but not at the expense of your mental well-being. Moreover, this story is a call for you to balance your empathy with common sense, ensuring that your relationships are mutually nurturing rather than one-sided. Cultivating a sense of self-preservation alongside your natural inclination to help others is imperative. Anna's story serves as a powerful reminder that setting boundaries is not a sign of a lack of empathy but a necessary step toward maintaining a healthy and respectful relationship, both with yourself and with others.

The Perils of Identifying Too Much With Empathy

Without a doubt, empathy is a wonderful and strong quality that enables individuals to connect and understand each other deeply. However, over-identifying with this component of your personality as an empath might leave you vulnerable, particularly when you are in relationships with narcissists. This section examines the dangers of over-identifying as empathic and how it may result in exploitation.

An over-identification with empathy might lead to a tendency to define yourself solely in terms of your empathy. This self-concept can become so ingrained that you might feel compelled to constantly act on your empathic impulses, often at the expense of your well-being. Because you believe it is your responsibility to be the caregiver or the understanding partner, you may find yourself in circumstances where you give too much, put aside your own needs, and overlook warning signs in relationships. This over-identification can also lead to a skewed sense of responsibility for others' emotions and actions. You might believe that you must solve people's problems or maintain peace at all costs. This belief can be particularly dangerous when dealing with a narcissist, who may manipulate this sense of responsibility to their advantage. They can play on your guilt and sense of duty, knowing that you are likely to go above and beyond to help, even if it puts your health at risk.

Losing personal boundaries is another concern associated with over-identifying with your empathic nature. It could be hard for you to say no or to see when someone is taking advantage of your kindness since you want to connect and help. Narcissists are skilled at pushing boundaries, and if you do not set clear boundaries, you could find yourself easily taken advantage of by their manipulative tactics.

Furthermore, over-identification with empathy may result in emotional burnout. It can be draining to continuously experience and absorb other people's emotions, especially when self-care is lacking. It is crucial to keep in mind that having empathy does not mean you have to be available and open to everyone all the time. You must take time for yourself, to recharge and to engage in activities that bring joy and relaxation.

You need to develop a balanced understanding of your empathic nature to reduce these risks. Understand that your empathy is not your entire identity; rather, it is only one aspect of who you are. Recognize when to set healthy boundaries and understand that it is okay to prioritize your own needs and well-being. Recall that taking care of yourself just ensures you have the energy and resources to be empathic when it truly matters, not that it lessens your empathy.

Meet Sarah, a dedicated social worker, and a natural empath. Sarah's ability to feel and understand the emotions of her clients made her exceptional at her job. But in her personal life, she started to see a concerning pattern. Sarah kept finding herself drawn to narcissistic partners in her relationships. These partners would often exhibit intense emotions and a need for her constant support, which Sarah felt compelled to provide due to her empathic nature. In her most recent relationship with Michael, a charming but self-centered individual, Sarah found herself giving endlessly. Michael would often share stories of his troubled past and current struggles, eliciting Sarah's sympathy and support. Sarah often put her wants and well-being last since she believed it was her duty to support him. Sarah's friends and family noticed that she was getting more and more exhausted and depressed over time. They pointed out that Michael hardly ever seemed to care about her or take her wants into account. But Sarah believed that regardless of the cost to herself, it was her responsibility as an empath to understand and support. Sarah did not start to see things more clearly until she got to the point of emotional exhaustion. She realized that her over-identification with being an empath had led her to ignore her own needs and boundaries. This revelation marked a turning point for Sarah. She began to concentrate on setting boundaries and practicing self-care to counterbalance her innate empathy. She became aware of when she was giving too much and started to understand that she was not in charge of saving or healing her partner.

You can see how crucial it is to avoid using your empathy to define who you are by looking at Sarah's experience. It serves as a reminder that although empathy is an admirable quality, your happiness and well-being should not suffer because of it. Sarah's story emphasizes how important it is for you to maintain your boundaries and understand that caring for yourself is not selfish but rather necessary for a healthy and balanced life. This scenario should prompt you to consider your inclinations toward over-identifying with empathy. It pushes you to strike a balance between looking out for other people and looking after yourself so that your empathy serves as a strength rather than a means of self-destruction.

Understanding Narcissistic Lures and How to Avoid Them

Empaths must recognize and avoid the subtle manipulations used by narcissists. This section is dedicated to helping you identify early warning signs of narcissistic behavior and provides strategies to protect your emotional well-being.

When dealing with a narcissist, one of the first warning signs is their tendency to shower you with a lot of attention and praise. This may manifest as an overabundance of praise, a laser-like concentration on your positive qualities, or a rapid push toward a deep emotional bond. Although it may be alluring to revel in this praise, narcissists frequently employ it as a tactic to quickly secure your affection and loyalty. Watch out for how fast a narcissist seeks to establish a close relationship with you. They may express strong feelings or push for a serious commitment unusually early, creating a false sense of intimacy. This fast tempo can be confusing, and it is frequently a calculated move to get closer before you have had a chance to get to know them.

The charm of a narcissist can be another deceptive lure. They often use their charisma to attract and engage others. But often this charm belies a lack of true understanding. Keep an eye on how they engage with other people, particularly in situations where they have nothing to gain. Signs of empathy deficit might include indifference to others' feelings, arrogance, or a failure to acknowledge others' successes genuinely. It is crucial to approach new relationships cautiously to protect yourself. Give yourself enough time to get a true sense of the person's personality and actions in different situations. It is essential to follow your instincts if something does not feel right; trust your gut.

Boundaries frequently cause narcissists to respond adversely. It is a serious red flag if you observe someone constantly pushing your boundaries or acting disrespectfully toward you. Mutual respect and understanding are the foundation of healthy relationships, and anyone who disregards your boundaries is not treating you with the respect you deserve. Establishing and maintaining clear boundaries is crucial. Be firm about your limits and communicate them. This is about identifying your comfort zone and making sure that boundaries are respected, not only about saying no.

Rely on your family and friends for support. They can offer a different perspective and help you identify warning signs that you might miss. When you are unsure, the people you care about can help and guide you.

Lastly, concentrate on increasing your self-awareness and self-esteem. The more confident you feel about yourself, the less susceptible you are to other people's manipulative behavior. Never forget that you deserve a relationship built on equality, respect, and genuine affection. You can escape the emotional pitfalls that come with getting involved with a narcissist and build healthy relationships by being aware of these warning signs and taking precautions to protect yourself.

How Empaths Can Build Resilience

As an empath, your journey through life is very profound. You experience the world with a depth of emotion that can be both your greatest asset and your most challenging burden. You need to understand how fostering emotional resilience can safeguard your well-being while allowing you to maintain your empathic nature.

To you, emotional resilience is developing an inner fortitude that gets you through the emotional storms you face regularly. It is about building a solid, stable foundation that allows you to feel empathy without being overwhelmed by it, not about hardening your heart or shutting yourself off to other people's emotions. Think of emotional resilience as a storm-resistant tree. Despite feeling the intensity of the wind, it sways with it and does not break. Similarly, it is possible to learn to feel and take in emotions without becoming overwhelmed by them. Because of your resilience, you can assist and empathize with others while being detached from their experiences and being fully present for their happiness or suffering.

You must acknowledge the distinct ways in which you feel emotions if you are to develop this resilience. You may have a deeper sense of things than other people do, or you may notice nuances that others overlook. Although this sensitivity is an inherent aspect of your personality, it need not control your emotional well-being. You can begin to establish a boundary between experiencing an emotion and becoming overcome by it by being aware of and cognizant of your emotional tendencies. Understanding when you are starting to feel overwhelmed and knowing how to gently pull back are important skills in developing emotional resilience. This does not imply that you are denying the people in need of you or that you are not following your intuition. All it signifies is that you are checking in with yourself to make sure you are not taking on more than you can manage.

While empathy can be a useful tool for understanding and connecting with others, it should not come at the expense of your well-being. You may make sure that you can remain sympathetic and caring while simultaneously honoring and defending your own emotional needs by taking care of your emotional resilience. Remember this as you proceed: Emotional resilience is a continuous process that takes time to master. It is an ongoing process that you incorporate into your day-to-day activities. It is about allowing oneself to fully feel but also providing the resources and fortitude you need to prosper in an emotionally demanding world.

Chapter 3:
Unveiling Narcissistic Manipulation

How Love-Bombing Works

L et us imagine the following scenario: You meet someone who appears to be the ideal partner in every way. They show you so much affection, attention, and admiration. It has the feel of a fast-moving fairy tale romance. This is a common narcissistic approach called "love-bombing," which is meant to knock you flat. However, underlying this seductive exterior lurks a deceptive motive that empaths may find especially harmful. An intentional display of extreme affection, attention, and admiration aimed at controlling or influencing another individual is known as love-bombing. In the eyes of a narcissist, this is a calculated move to swiftly establish their dominance in a power dynamic rather than an act of real love or concern. They form an emotional bond that is hard to break through grand gestures, flattery, and intense communication.

Love-bombing can work particularly well for empaths, who usually give people the benefit of the doubt and thrive on strong emotional relationships. It can seem like a dream come true to an empath because they are naturally drawn to people who seem to be so deeply in love with them. Because of their compassionate nature, empaths may be oblivious to warning signs that indicate this excessive attention is unhealthy or abnormal.

The dynamics of love-bombing entail a rapid escalation of the relationship. The narcissist will frequently push for serious commitment and exclusivity right away. After just a few dates, they might discuss their future together, giving off the impression that this is a "meant-to-be" relationship. This intensity can be quite alluring, and it can give an empath a sense of responsibility and connection that is hard to step away from. Love-bombing, though, is unsustainable. The excessive affection and attention will probably stop once the narcissist feels confident in their dominance over the relationship, leaving the empath confused and bereft. This abrupt change can be emotionally upsetting, making the empath wonder what they did wrong to cause such a drastic change.

Empaths need to be aware of and understand the love-bombing tactic. It is important to recognize that healthy relationships require time to establish and are built on mutual respect and understanding rather than overwhelming and immediate intensity. It could be time to stand back and give the matter a more thorough evaluation if you discover that your relationship is progressing too quickly.

Playing the Victim

Playing the victim is a manipulative strategy that narcissists frequently use. This tactic works especially well against empaths, who are compelled to help and heal others. For those who often find themselves taking care of others, it is important to understand how narcissists utilize this strategy to control and manipulate.

Fundamentally, playing the victim is when a narcissist, regardless of the reality, presents themselves as the injured party in a variety of scenarios. This portrayal is a premeditated tactic to influence those around them, especially empaths, rather than an attempt to communicate genuine hurt or find a way to work things out. Narcissists use victimization to gain control over others, avoid taking responsibility, and elicit sympathy. The need to assist someone who seems to be in need can be almost irresistible for empaths. Empaths have a great desire to ease other people's suffering and a profound feeling of compassion. Playing the victim allows narcissists to access these empathic traits, which frequently gives the empath the impression that they are in a unique position to offer the narcissist the support and understanding they require.

Although this dynamic can establish a strong emotional bond, that bond is predicated on manipulation. "Rescuing" the narcissist may provide the empath with a heightened sense of purpose or connection. This rescue effort is not without its difficulties, though. The goal of the narcissist's exaggerated or entirely fabricated victimization narrative is to maintain the empath's psychological and emotional attachment.

This strategy works well because it takes away the empath's natural guardedness and cynicism. An empath's natural reaction is to provide compassion and support to someone who appears to be suffering. This reaction may take precedence over their capacity for objectivity, particularly if the narcissist is adept at weaving a convincing narrative of victimhood. Furthermore, the empath may experience a cycle of obligation and guilt as a result of this strategy. The narcissist might say it outright or hint that the empath is the only person who can relate to them or provide comfort. This can put a great deal of emotional strain on the empath, who could feel in charge of the narcissist's welfare and caught in a never-ending loop of trying to appease and comfort them.

Empaths must be able to spot this kind of manipulation when it occurs. Persistent victimization is concerning, particularly when it is combined with a tendency to blame others and a lack of accountability. Healthy relationships do not have one person playing the victim all the time; instead, they require mutual support and accountability.

It might be enlightening to consider these questions during your interactions to help you determine whether someone is truly in need or is using victimhood as a manipulative tool:

- Reflect on their stories. Are they always portrayed as the victim, seemingly helpless in various situations?

- When they talk about past conflicts or issues, do they ever acknowledge their own role, or is it always someone else's fault?

- Do you feel a strong urge to rescue or save this person? Notice if your interactions leave you feeling overly responsible for their well-being.

- How do they speak about others? Is there a consistent pattern of blaming others for their problems?

- Consider how your interactions with this person affect you emotionally. Are you left feeling drained or burdened?

- Do they seem to use your empathy to validate their narrative of perpetual victimhood?

- Observe their reaction when you set boundaries or are unable to provide the support they seek. Is there a negative reaction or an increase in victim-playing?

You may tell if the person you are interacting with is a narcissist who is using victim-playing as a strategy for manipulation by asking yourself these questions. Understanding this tactic is essential to preventing the exploitation of your empathic nature in a relationship dynamic in which one partner is constantly the victim and the other is constantly the rescuer.

The Tactics and Effects of Gaslighting

Narcissists frequently employ the subtle yet sneaky tactic of gaslighting, which can have a significant negative impact on empaths. By rejecting facts, their surroundings, or their emotions, one might undermine the reality of another person. Gaslighting can be extremely confusing and harmful for empaths, who deeply trust their feelings and intuition. Gaslighting is fundamentally a control tactic. This is a method used by narcissists to make you feel unstable and confused, leading you to question your perceptions and memories. This may cause you to lose confidence in your judgment and increase your reliance on the narcissist's version of reality.

Think about the ways that gaslighting could manifest in a conversation. If you bring up a concern or an issue, the narcissist may claim the event never happened or that you are recalling details incorrectly. When you share your feelings, they might say you are overly sensitive or dramatic. You may eventually start to doubt your own experiences and feelings as a result of this ongoing denial of your reality. For empaths, gaslighting can have a profound psychological effect. Being continuously reminded that your feelings are incorrect or invalid can be extremely unsettling if you are someone who relies on intuition and feels emotions deeply. It may cause you to feel alone, and anxious, and to stop believing in other people and yourself.

It is critical to keep a strong sense of self and faith in your judgment to guard against gaslighting. One useful tool for validating your experiences is to keep a record of the things you do and the people you talk to. Having a support system of friends or family members who can validate your reality and provide an unbiased viewpoint is also essential. Furthermore, being aware of the warning indications of gaslighting can enable you to spot it when it occurs. Frequently questioning yourself, feeling as if you are apologizing all the time, and feeling perplexed during conversations with the individual are some common indicators.

Never forget that your experiences and feelings are real. You cannot sustain your mental and emotional health if you do not trust your reality. Seeking assistance from a mental health professional can be a crucial first step toward recovery and confidence restoration if you discover that you are being gaslighted.

To better understand the subtle and detrimental effects of gaslighting, let us examine a real-life scenario involving an empath named Emma and her narcissistic partner, Alex. Emma, who is intuitive and empathic by nature, became more confused as she interacted with Alex. Little things at first, like Alex denying saying something Emma could recall him saying or brushing aside her emotions over particular topics as if she was being overly sensitive or misinterpreting the situation. Emma, for example, once expressed concern about Alex's recent lack of communication. Alex vehemently disputed that his behavior had changed, claiming Emma was imagining things. He even went as far as to question her memory of past events, insinuating that she often made things up. Emma was perplexed and began to question her perceptions as a result. These instances became more common over time. Emma discovered that she was continuously doubting her feelings and memories. Because Alex had persuaded her that her friends and family did not share his understanding of her, she began to feel isolated. Her dependence on Alex's perception of reality only grew as a result of her isolation. Emma was significantly impacted psychologically. She began to experience anxiety and feel less confident in her judgment. Her once-trusted intuition appeared unreliable at this point. She felt stuck in a loop where she would try to prove her perceptions, only to be met with denial and dismissal.

This scenario illustrates the damaging effects of gaslighting, especially on empaths. Emma's natural tendency to empathize and seek deep connections was exploited by Alex's manipulation, leaving her questioning her reality. Emma's story makes it very evident how crucial it is to have faith in your perceptions and feelings. Reaffirming your reality might be helped by keeping a record of events and conversations. Maintaining connections with friends and family can also offer the outside affirmation and encouragement required to offset the effects of gaslighting.

By considering these questions, you can determine whether you are being gaslighted in any of your relationships:

- Have you ever felt that someone is deliberately trying to make you doubt your memory or perception of events?

- Do you frequently find yourself questioning your feelings or beliefs because someone insists that you are wrong or misremembering things?

- After conversations with a particular person, do you often feel more confused and less confident about your thoughts and feelings?

- Is there a pattern where you express your feelings or concerns, only to be told that you are overreacting or being too sensitive?

- Do you notice a tendency in someone to dismiss or trivialize your experiences, making you feel like your reality is not valid?

- Are there moments where you feel isolated or alone in your perceptions as if no one else would understand or believe you?

- When you share your thoughts or memories with a specific individual, do they often counter them with their version of events, making you feel as though you cannot trust your mind?

The purpose of these questions is to assist you in recognizing the subtle indicators of gaslighting. Because they mostly depend on their emotions and instincts, empaths may be especially vulnerable to this kind of manipulation. Being able to spot gaslighting is essential to preserving your sense of self and trust in your perceptions.

The Narcissist's Toolbox: Lying, Shaming, and Guilt Trips

Have you ever had the feeling that you are constantly walking on eggshells, never knowing quite what the next reality will bring? This is frequently what people caught in a narcissist's manipulative web go through. Lying, shaming, and guilt trips are among their arsenal of tools, but they are more than just tactics; they are weapons meant to control, confuse, and destabilize, and they work especially well against the empath's compassionate nature.

Lying: Imagine that during a conversation, you remember specific details clearly, yet the narcissist openly denies them, telling you that you are wrong. This is a calculated maneuver to keep you off balance, not merely a case of forgetfulness. A narcissist's ability to lie might cause you to doubt your memory and sanity and rewrite reality. It is essential to trust your own experiences to combat this. Keeping a journal can be a useful tool for validating your memories and giving you a solid ground of facts if someone questions your reality.

Shaming: Imagine receiving subtle criticism that makes you feel inadequate about your decisions or personality. Shaming is a tactic used by narcissists to undermine your self-esteem and increase your reliance on their approval. Use self-affirmation techniques to counter this. Remind yourself of your accomplishments and worth. As a counter-narrative to the shame, surround yourself with positive people.

Guilt Trips: Think back to the times you were made to feel bad for voicing your wants or making choices that did not suit the narcissist's preferences. The purpose of guilt trips is to coerce you into obeying. Defined boundaries are essential in this situation. Affirm your right to make the decisions that are best for you to learn how to recognize and reject emotional manipulation.

It takes a combination of self-awareness, self-worth affirmation, and rigorous boundary-setting to successfully navigate these strategies. You can begin to break their hold on your emotions and reactions by becoming aware of and recognizing these behaviors. Regaining your reality, your self-worth, and your freedom from the controlling grasp of a narcissist are the goals of this journey.

Strategies for Control: Invalidation and the Silent Treatment

The act of dismissing or belittling your thoughts, feelings, or experiences is known as invalidation. It is an attempt to get you to doubt the validity of your emotions. Imagine telling someone you were experiencing something, and getting comments like, "You are overreacting," or "You are just too sensitive." This kind of response might gradually undermine your self-confidence by making you question your own emotions and be reluctant to express them in the future.

In contrast, the silent treatment entails the narcissist ignoring or excluding you. Given that it frequently occurs suddenly and sometimes follows periods of closeness, this behavior can be particularly upsetting and unpleasant. The silent treatment is intended to dominate and punish, fostering an environment of fear and uncertainty. Even in situations where you are not at fault, you may find yourself apologizing or changing your behavior to reestablish contact.

These strategies can be especially harmful to empaths, who experience emotions deeply. They may result in emotions such as isolation, anxiety, and a sense of being unworthy of attention or love.

Because empaths naturally desire harmony and understanding, they may be more susceptible to emotional manipulation techniques.

It is critical to identify these strategies for what they are—control tactics—to deal with them. Reaffirming your feelings and grounding yourself in your reality are essential while dealing with invalidation. Having a network of friends or relatives who can offer emotional support and a reality check might be beneficial. On the other hand, the secret to handling the silent treatment with a narcissist is to resist the urge to seek the narcissist's approval. Focus on activities and relationships that make you happy and reinforce your self-worth. Remember that the silent treatment does not indicate your value; rather, it is a reflection of the narcissist's need for control.

The following questions can assist in recognizing and understanding these tactics, aiding in your emotional clarity and resilience:

- Have you experienced moments where your feelings or thoughts were dismissed or belittled when expressing them to someone? Think about how these instances made you feel and their impact on your willingness to share in the future.

- Recall any periods when someone close to you abruptly stopped communicating, leaving you in a state of confusion and anxiety. How did these instances of the silent treatment affect your emotional well-being and your responses to that person?

- Consider whether you find yourself doubting the validity of your emotions or experiences after interactions with a certain individual. This could indicate a pattern of invalidation, where your reality is consistently undermined.

- Reflect on your reactions when faced with the silent treatment. Do you notice a tendency to seek reconciliation, possibly at the expense of your feelings and needs?

- Are there recurring patterns in your relationship where expressing your needs or concerns leads to emotional withdrawal rather than resolution? This might suggest the use of the silent treatment as a manipulation tool.

- Think about your feelings when you are away from the person who often invalidates or ignores you. Do you feel a sense of relief or freedom? This reaction can be indicative of the emotional strain you might be experiencing.

Chapter 4:
Getting Out of the Abuse Cycle

Understanding the Narcissistic Abuse Cycle

Y ou need to be aware of the abusive cycle that frequently underlies these interactions. Idealization, devaluation, and discarding are the three stages that this cycle usually goes through. Every stage has a distinct impact on you as an empath and contributes to the narcissist's manipulative tactics.

During the idealization stage, the narcissist may try to put you on a pedestal. Intense romance, affection, and attention are characteristics of this stage. It can seem like a whirlwind, full of extravagant gestures and promises of love. This stage may appear like the profound, meaningful relationship you have been waiting for as an empath. But you must understand that this is frequently a calculated action on the part of the narcissist to win your affection and trust, leaving you more open to manipulation in the future.

The devaluation phase can be a startling one to enter. That same partner who used to be so loving and admiring of you could turn into someone who is emotionally abusive, cold, and critical. You may find this time to be quite confusing and painful. You may start to doubt your worth and the reality of the relationship due to the sharp contrast between the affection you formerly experienced and the cruel actions presently being directed toward you. You may put more effort into trying to win back the narcissist's affection, frequently at the expense of your well-being.

The discarding stage might eventually come. At this point, the narcissist may decide to suddenly break up with you or stop showing affection because they believe you are no longer able to meet their needs. You might feel worthless and abandoned at this phase. But if the narcissist feels you are becoming stronger or more independent, it is normal for them to go back to the idealization stage.

When considering the cycle of narcissistic abuse in more detail, Jenna's story provides a striking example of this destructive pattern. Since Jenna is an empathic person, she could not help but be pulled to Marcus, who at first glance seemed like the perfect match. Marcus represented all that was charming and loving throughout the idealization stage. He was so attentive to Jenna, and he seemed to get her. For an empath who feeds on emotional connection, Jenna felt valued and cherished, a feeling that resonates deeply. However once the relationship entered the devaluation phase, things drastically changed. Marcus became different. He started criticizing Jenna for unimportant things, which made her feel less confident. His once-kind remarks evolved into critical assessments. Feeling bewildered and hurt, Jenna sought to change her behavior in an attempt to win back Marcus' loving attention. The discarding phase brought even more pain. Marcus withdrew his affection, leaving Jenna feeling abandoned and questioning her worth. Despite the emotional turmoil, Jenna found herself hoping for a return to the idealization phase, a hope that kept her tied to the cycle.

Jenna's story is a stark reminder of how the cycle of narcissistic abuse unfolds. It highlights the emotional roller coaster that empaths often experience in such relationships—the intense connection followed by confusion, self-doubt, and a longing for the affection that was once so freely given. Understanding this cycle through Jenna's experience can be eye-opening. It emphasizes how crucial it is to identify these stages as components of a planned pattern of abuse rather than as variations in a normal relationship. For you, as an empath, this understanding is crucial in identifying similar patterns in your relationships and taking steps to protect your emotional well-being. Despite all of its difficulties, Jenna's journey also shows the power and resiliency that may arise from confronting and acknowledging the reality of narcissistic abuse.

Identifying and Handling Red Flags

You must identify the early warning indicators, or "red flags," in any relationship, but particularly in one with a potential narcissist. These signs frequently indicate the start of a destructive cycle of abuse. You can safeguard yourself from becoming intricately involved in a toxic relationship by being aware of these warning signals and understanding how to react to them.

Red Flag 1: Intensity and Rushing the Relationship

The intensity of the relationship is one of the first warning signs. A narcissist could rush into a deep connection, making hasty declarations of love or pushing for commitment. Although this may sound nice, it is usually a ploy to quickly establish control. If you find yourself caught up in this whirlwind, stand back and give yourself some space to evaluate the relationship at a more realistic pace.

Red Flag 2: Constant Need for Admiration and Validation

Narcissists are driven by an unquenchable desire for admiration and validation. Your partner may have narcissistic traits if they are always looking for praise, react badly to criticism, or want special treatment. Setting limits in these situations is crucial to avoid giving in to their incessant demand for approval.

Red Flag 3: Lack of Empathy

A lack of genuine empathy is a hallmark of narcissistic behavior. If you notice that your partner seems indifferent to your feelings or the feelings of others, this is a significant red flag. Recognizing this trait can help you understand that their emotional responses—or lack thereof—are not a reflection of your worth.

Red Flag 4: Manipulation and Gaslighting

Gaslighting and manipulation are two strategies frequently employed by narcissists. These are major warning signs if you discover that your partner frequently twists your words, plays emotional games, or makes you doubt your reality. You can recognize and deal with these manipulative actions by trusting your instincts and looking for external perspectives.

Red Flag 5: Past Relationship Patterns

A narcissist's previous relationships can frequently expose behavioral patterns. If they talk badly about all of their past relationships, always putting themselves in the victim role, this may be a sign of how they may treat you in the future. Understanding these stories can provide insights into their relationship dynamics.

Red Flag 6: Jealousy and Possessiveness

Excessive jealousy and possessiveness are classic warning signs. When your partner attempts to distance you from friends and family or becomes overly concerned about how you behave with them, these acts are not signs of affection but rather of a need for control.

Red Flag 7: Frequent Mood Swings or Explosive Anger

If your partner exhibits unpredictable mood swings or excessive rage over little matters, proceed with caution. Narcissists frequently utilize environments of uncertainty and anxiety to stay in control, and this instability can contribute to those conditions.

Red Flag 8: Playing the Victim

Narcissists often portray themselves as the perpetual victim. It is a warning indication that your partner may be manipulating and trying to elicit sympathy if they constantly place the blame for their problems on other people while refusing to accept accountability for their actions.

Red Flag 9: Disrespecting Your Boundaries

Your boundaries may be routinely tested or disregarded by a narcissist. This could manifest as someone ignoring your opinions, invading your privacy, or not respecting your physical space. Mutual respect is the foundation of a healthy relationship, and disrespecting boundaries is a surefire way to get into difficulties.

Red Flag 10: Inconsistent Behavior and Broken Promises

Keep an eye out for inconsistent behavior and broken promises. If your partner frequently breaks promises or behaves in a way that is inconsistent with their words, these acts may be a sign of a lack of integrity and respect.

Red Flag 11: Constant Criticism and Belittlement

It is a serious warning indicator if you discover that your partner constantly criticizes you—even for insignificant things—and belittles your achievements or dreams. This unceasing criticism may be a ploy to make you feel less confident in yourself and more dependent on their approval.

Red Flag 12: Overstepping Personal Information Boundaries

A narcissist could ask too many personal questions or insist on knowing information that makes you uncomfortable. This invasion of privacy is concerning since it shows a lack of respect for your boundaries and autonomy.

Red Flag 13: Public Humiliation or Embarrassment

Observe your partner's behavior in social or public settings. If they frequently—either subtly or overtly—make fun of you in front of other people, it is a strategy they use to establish control over how other people see you and demonstrate their dominance.

Red Flag 14: Financial Control or Exploitation

Another concern is financial control. Economic abuse occurs when your partner takes charge of your money, makes important financial decisions without your permission, or puts financial pressure on you to gain power and control over you.

Red Flag 15: Disregard for Your Emotional or Physical Well-Being

It is concerning when your partner consistently disregards your mental or physical health. This could show up as physical abuse, neglecting your needs, or simply disinterest in your feelings.

Red Flag 16: Isolation From Friends and Family

Narcissists may attempt to cut you off from your support system. It is a warning sign if you observe that your partner inhibits or discourages your social interactions with friends and relatives. This isolation is a control tactic to make you more reliant on them.

Red Flag 17: Inconsistent Commitment

Be cautious of a partner who fluctuates in their feelings. If they are passionate and committed one moment and distant or non-committal the next, this inconsistency can be a tactic to keep you off-balance and emotionally invested in seeking their approval.

Red Flag 18: Using Guilt as a Weapon

Guilt is a common tool used by narcissists to coerce you into doing what they want. It is a serious red flag if you often find yourself feeling bad about things that are not your fault or if your partner uses guilt to override your decisions.

Red Flag 19: Disrespect for Your Time and Efforts

Check to see whether your partner frequently treats your time and efforts with indifference. This could show up as their constant expectation that you adapt to their schedule, their disdain for your commitments, or their lack of appreciation for the effort you put into the relationship.

Red Flag 20: Excessive Control Over Daily Activities

Having too much control over your everyday routine is not a good thing. It is an indication of controlling behavior when your partner makes unreasonable demands about what you should wear, eat, or do with your time.

Why Red Flags Should Never Be Ignored

Hope or the desire to see the best in someone are often the reasons behind ignoring red flags. Believing that love is stronger than everything else, empaths may find themselves justifying or rationalizing a partner's destructive behavior. However, this approach can result in a vicious circle of abuse and manipulation, with grave emotional and occasionally physical harm. Ignoring these warning signs could land you in a relationship that slowly saps your independence, happiness, and self-esteem. It can become more difficult to leave or to recognize your worth the longer you stay in such a relationship. It is similar to being in a fog when you are getting farther away from self-realization and clarity with every step.

It is not only about avoiding toxic relationships when you recognize and act upon red flags; it is also about empowering yourself. With this understanding, you will be able to set boundaries and understand what you deserve in a relationship. It is about changing the narrative from one of victimhood to one of strength and self-respect. Recognizing these warning signs also helps you develop a clearer sense of what a healthy relationship looks like. It enables you to discern between genuine affection and love and manipulative strategies masquerading as love. Building and maintaining nurturing, respectful, and supportive relationships requires this clarity.

Armed with the knowledge of these red flags, you can approach new relationships with a more informed perspective. You get better at spotting behaviors that do not align with your values and needs. This does not mean you approach every relationship with suspicion; rather, it means you engage with a heightened sense of awareness and self-respect. Healthy relationships have mutual give-and-take, open and courteous communication, and respected boundaries. You can avoid relationships that do not provide these fundamental qualities by identifying red flags. Not only does this keep you safe, but it creates room for more fulfilling and meaningful relationships.

Ending the Toxic Cycle

Starting the process of breaking out from the cycle of a toxic relationship—especially one with a narcissist—is a significant step toward reclaiming your life. It is a road that calls for courage, resilience, and an unwavering belief in your worth. There are techniques to help and guide you through this difficult but liberating process.

First and foremost, you must acknowledge the extraordinary power you already possess just by considering this change. This acknowledgment is a powerful realization of your resilience and capability, not only self-affirmation. After enduring, you are now prepared to close this chapter of your life and begin a new one that will hopefully bring you greater respect, peace, and fulfillment.

Imagining a future free from the toxicity of your current relationship is a vital step. What does this future look like for you? How do you feel in this envisioned life? This is not mere daydreaming; it is a process of constructing a hopeful and tangible future—a life where you are valued and your needs are met. Allow this vision to serve as your beacon of hope while you navigate the challenges that lie ahead.

Determining your non-negotiables is essential to this journey. You are no longer prepared to make compromises in these areas of your life or your relationships. They create your bill of rights and act as a continual reminder of your expectations and standards in relationships. These non-negotiables—emotional support, honesty, and respect for one another—will help you stay grounded in your decision to break free from the toxic cycle. During this period, self-compassion is your ally. The path to liberation is not easy to travel; it is paved with obstacles and emotional hurdles. Show compassion and empathy to yourself. Embrace the moments of doubt or guilt with the same empathy you would offer a beloved friend. Not only can this self-compassion provide comfort, but it also serves as a source of strength to get you through difficult times.

Finding resources that empower you can help further. These resources—whether they come from books, online forums, or support groups—offer advice, tactics, and the comforting knowledge that you are not traveling this path alone. These are resources that can provide you with the information and techniques you need to break free from the toxic cycle. Remember that breaking free consists of taking tiny, steady steps. Every step you take—no matter how small—is a step closer to your new life. Celebrate these steps as they contribute to the journey toward a life where you are respected and free. Your support system is invaluable during this time. Friends, family, or a trusted therapist can provide the encouragement and perspective you need. They serve as a sounding board for you, providing comfort and a reminder of the bright future that awaits.

Finally, reestablishing a connection with your interests and passions is a beautiful way to rediscover who you are. These activities are more than just hobbies; they are expressions of your individuality—aspects of yourself that the relationship might have obscured. They serve as essential components of the happy life you are pursuing and are reminders of who you are outside of the toxic cycle.

While breaking the cycle of a toxic relationship is certainly difficult, doing so is a powerful step toward respect, self-love, and a happier future. Every stride you take is an indication of your strength and a move toward a life filled with respect and happiness you deserve.

First Steps Toward Healing From Narcissistic Abuse

Healing from a narcissistic relationship is similar to gradually waking up from a long, disorienting fog. You may experience a range of feelings during this period, from relief and liberation to confusion and sorrow. This time is not simply for healing; it is a profound journey of rediscovering who you are and what truly matters to you. Exiting a narcissistic relationship might leave you with a complicated emotional terrain. It is important to allow yourself to fully experience this emotional spectrum. It is acceptable to feel hurt, upset, angry, or even to have second thoughts about your choice in a relationship you believed you had. Though they are a natural byproduct of the healing process, these emotions do not define your journey.

Reestablishing contact with your inner self is an essential part of this journey. It is time to rediscover what makes you, you, after being in a relationship where your identity and needs may have taken a back seat. This could entail pursuing new interests or going back to old hobbies that you put aside. It is about honoring your true self and paying attention to your inner voice. Creating a personal narrative is an effective healing technique. This narrative is your story, told from a perspective that recognizes your resilience and strength. It is not about reliving the past but about understanding how your experiences have shaped you. Any kind of expression, including journaling, art, and writing, can be therapeutic. It is a means of processing your journey and acknowledging how far you have come.

It is essential to have a growth-oriented and self-compassionate mindset. There will be setbacks and days when it seems like you are not progressing; healing is not a linear process. It is critical to treat oneself with kindness during these trying times. Though it may not seem like it at times, acknowledge that every day is a step closer to recovery.

Rediscovering passion and joy in life is another step in the healing process. Take part in things that light up your spirit and make you happy. These activities are more than just hobbies; they are affirmations of your independence and joy, regardless of whether it is a new activity you have always wanted to explore or one you have always loved. Developing meaningful connections with other people is equally important. Look for relationships and communities where you are valued and understood. Mutual respect and understanding should be the foundation of these relationships, allowing you to be who you truly are without fear of judgment. Lastly, making plans for the future can help direct your path to recovery. How do you envision your life to be? What kind of relationships are you hoping to foster? These intentions are reflections of your deepest desires and aspirations, not just goals.

The journey to recovery from narcissistic abuse is a profoundly personal and life-changing one. It is about finding yourself again, understanding your worth, and creating a life that reflects who you truly are. Remember that a better, more authentic future is ahead of you and that you have the power to heal.

The Cost of Remaining in a Toxic Relationship

Realizing the costs of continuing in a toxic relationship is more than simply being aware of the dangers; it also gives you the power to make the right decisions now to improve your future. This realization serves as a trigger for change in you—a call to action that emphasizes the importance of your happiness and well-being.

Although substantial, the psychological and emotional toll of a toxic relationship is not insurmountable. You have what it takes to overcome this problem. In a situation like that, your self-worth may be undermined daily, but keep in mind that it is intrinsic and unchangeable. The difficulties you encounter in these relationships are not nearly as strong as your perseverance. Embracing this truth is the first step in reclaiming your power. Physical health, often compromised due to the stress of a toxic relationship, can be restored. Your body's ability to heal is remarkable, and with the decision to leave toxicity behind, you begin a journey toward better health and vitality. This journey is proof of your body's resilience and your commitment to self-care.

Social connections and relationships that may have weakened can be rebuilt. Those who genuinely love you will support you in this courageous change. Reaching out to friends and family, or even forming new connections, can reignite the sense of community and belonging that everyone deserves.

Even though they might have taken a backseat, your personal and professional goals still matter. This is your chance to put your aspirations and ambitions back into sharp focus. Although they are manifestations of your skills and interests, your career and personal accomplishments do not define you. Reaching your full potential can be achieved by taking back these areas of your life.

It is possible to mend the emotional damage caused by a toxic relationship. This healing journey is an opportunity for profound personal growth. In the long run, this practice can help you develop stronger boundaries, a deeper sense of self, and more fulfilling relationships. Your resilience, empathy, and self-awareness have increased as a result of the priceless lessons you have learned.

If one's financial independence has been compromised, it can be restored. This is your chance to regain independence by taking charge of your finances. Achieving financial autonomy strengthens your independence and is a liberating and empowering journey.

Knowing the cost of staying in a toxic relationship is a powerful motivator. It is an exhortation to value yourself, put your health and happiness first, and take the required actions to ensure a better, more fulfilling future. You are capable, strong, and able to go past this chapter. You are in for a life full of growth, joy, and respect. Resolving to leave toxic relationships is a choice to live a life that truly reflects your worth.

Chapter 5:
An Empath's Battle With Codependency

Codependency in an Empath-Narcissist Dynamic

M eet Jane, an empath who became caught in a relationship with a narcissist named Ethan. Jane always prided herself on being understanding and compassionate, qualities that initially drew Ethan closer to her. Their relationship started as a whirlwind romance, with Ethan showering her with attention and affection. However, as time passed, Jane began to notice a disturbing pattern. Their relationship began to be dominated by Ethan's needs and problems. Jane found that she had to always put her needs and well-being last to satisfy him. In an attempt to relive the loving moments they once shared, she would cancel plans with friends to be with Ethan, put up with his mood swings, and apologize even when she was not at fault.

The codependency in an empath-narcissist dynamic is well illustrated in this scenario. Here, you can see how Jane's empathy led her to become more and more focused on meeting Ethan's needs at the expense of her own. This pattern is ingrained in Jane's emotional patterns and beliefs and is not limited to the actions she takes. In relationships like Jane's, your natural inclination to care and nurture can be exploited, creating an imbalance. Because of this exploitation, the narcissist's need for attention and validation gets in the way of your desire to help them, creating a vicious cycle. Like Jane, you may find yourself sacrificing your own needs to satisfy the narcissist, jeopardizing your well-being in the process.

Because narcissists are often manipulative and lack empathy, the dynamic in your relationship with them can be especially harmful. Your giving nature may be continuously taken advantage of, resulting in a one-sided relationship in which your needs and wants are never met. You must identify this codependent dynamic in your relationship. It is about seeing the signs of an unhealthy balance and understanding the psychological reasons behind this pattern. This recognition is crucial for you to start addressing and altering these codependent behaviors and laying the groundwork for healthier and more fulfilling relationships.

As you reflect on your relationships, consider how these dynamics manifest themselves in your interactions. Understanding and acknowledging the presence of codependency is the first step in moving toward a healthier balance in your relationships.

Let us look at some key questions that might assist you in recognizing similar codependent dynamics in your relationships. With the help of these questions, you should be able to identify and understand codependency patterns and make better decisions for yourself.

- Do you often find yourself prioritizing your partner's needs and emotions over your own? Reflect on times when you might have neglected your own needs or feelings to keep your partner happy or to maintain harmony in the relationship.

- Consider whether you find yourself constantly trying to "fix" or "save" your partner. Ask yourself if you feel responsible for your partner's well-being or happiness to the extent that it overshadows your own.

- Think about whether you fear expressing your true feelings or opinions in the relationship. Are there instances where you have held back from sharing your thoughts or feelings for fear of upsetting your partner or causing conflict?

- Assess if you feel guilty when taking time for yourself or pursuing your interests. Do you experience a sense of guilt or anxiety when focusing on your hobbies, interests, or self-care?

- Evaluate how difficult it is for you to set boundaries with your partner. Consider situations where you might have struggled to communicate your limits or felt that your boundaries were not respected.

- Reflect on whether you often feel responsible for your partner's actions or behaviors. Do you tend to take the blame for your partner's actions or feel the need to apologize on their behalf?

- Think about why you might be staying in the relationship despite feeling unhappy or unfulfilled. Consider the reasons for staying and whether these reasons are aligned with your true desires and well-being.

By considering these questions, you can identify codependent tendencies in your relationships. It is about realizing that, even while empathy and compassion are inherent qualities of who you are, you should not let them compromise your happiness and emotional well-being.

How to Tell Empathy From Codependency

Knowing and feeling other people's emotions on a profound level comes naturally to empaths. Even though this is a beautiful and rare gift, you need to discern between codependent tendencies and healthy empathic behavior. Making this distinction can help you avoid falling into harmful codependency patterns and instead have your empathic qualities enrich your relationships.

Empathy, in its healthiest form, is about being attuned to others' emotions and offering support without compromising your well-being. It involves a balanced exchange where your emotional needs are also met. Healthy empathy allows you to be compassionate and understanding while maintaining your boundaries and sense of self. Conversely, codependency occurs when your empathy drives you to constantly prioritize the needs of others over your own, frequently at your expense. It is characterized by an excessive emotional or psychological reliance on a partner, usually one who requires care or support due to illness, addiction, or other issues.

Key Differences:

1. Boundary Setting: In healthy empathy, you can offer support while maintaining clear boundaries. In codependency,

boundaries are often blurred or nonexistent, leading to over-involvement in your partner's problems.

2. Self-Identity: Healthy empathy allows you to retain a strong sense of self-identity. In codependent relationships, your identity and self-worth become heavily tied to your role in supporting or "saving" your partner.

3. Reciprocity: Empathic relationships are characterized by reciprocity and mutual respect. Codependent relationships are often one-sided, with the empath continuously giving and the partner taking.

4. Emotional Independence: While healthy empathy involves sharing emotions, it also includes emotional independence. In codependency, your emotional state becomes heavily dependent on your partner's mood and behavior.

5. Self-Care: Empaths in healthy relationships prioritize self-care and self-compassion. In codependent dynamics, self-care often takes a backseat to the needs of the partner.

It is imperative that you, as an empath, recognize the distinction between codependency and empathy. It helps you navigate relationships in a way that honors your empathic nature without falling into unhealthy patterns. Knowing these differences empowers you to engage in relationships that are nurturing, reciprocal, and respectful of your boundaries. As you reflect on your relationships, consider how these differences manifest in your interactions. Striving for a balance where your empathy enriches your relationships without leading to codependency is key to building fulfilling and healthy connections.

How to Spot Signs of Codependency in Yourself

Recognizing signs of codependency in yourself is a crucial step in fostering healthier relationships. As an empath, you might find it difficult to distinguish between codependency and your innate empathy. Here is a guide to help you evaluate yourself and spot codependency in your relationships:

1. Your Happiness Depends on Your Partner: Reflect on whether your mood and happiness are heavily influenced by your partner's state of mind or behavior. If you find your emotional well-being is closely tied to how your partner is feeling or acting, it might be a sign of codependency.

2. Difficulty Making Decisions Without Your Partner: Consider if making decisions—even small ones—feels daunting without your partner's input or approval. Codependency can manifest in an over-reliance on your partner for decision-making.

3. Neglecting Your Own Needs: Think about how often you put your own needs, interests, or well-being on the back burner to focus on your partner. Regularly neglecting your own needs for the sake of your partner is a common trait in codependent relationships.

4. Fear of Abandonment: Assess if there is a persistent fear of being abandoned or rejected by your partner. This fear can lead you to go to great lengths to keep them happy, often at your expense.

5. Feeling Responsible for Your Partner's Problems: Do you often feel like it is your duty to fix or solve your partner's problems? If you are taking on the responsibility for your partner's issues, it might indicate a codependent tendency.

6. Staying in the Relationship Despite Unhappiness: Reflect on why you are staying in the relationship. If you are staying out of fear, obligation, or the belief that you can change your partner, rather than genuine contentment and mutual respect, it is important to reconsider the dynamics of your relationship.

7. Your Self-Esteem is Tied to the Relationship: Consider whether your self-esteem is heavily influenced by your relationship. In codependency, self-worth often becomes intertwined with how you perceive your role and effectiveness in managing your partner's life or problems.

By asking yourself these questions and reflecting on your responses, you can start to identify patterns that may indicate codependency. Recognizing these signs is the first step toward making changes in how you approach relationships. It is about finding a balance where your empathic qualities are expressed healthily, without losing sight of your own needs and well-being.

How to Break Free From Codependent Patterns

Let us talk about reshaping the way you engage in relationships, moving away from codependency toward a more balanced interaction. This change is not just about altering a few behaviors; it is a deeper transformation that touches the core of how you relate to others and yourself.

Begin by viewing empathy as a capacity for understanding and connection rather than as a duty to bear the emotional burdens of others. This allows empathy to exist without requiring self-sacrifice. It is similar to having superpowers, only you know when to use them and when to let go. This understanding allows you to offer support without being overwhelmed in the process. Reflect on your relationships. Are there moments where you feel lost in the needs and emotions of others? These moments serve as gentle reminders for you to pause and consider your own needs. It is like being in a dance where sometimes you lead, and sometimes you follow, but you never stop listening to the rhythm of your own steps. Setting boundaries may not come naturally to you at first, particularly if you are accustomed to always saying "yes." However, see it as drawing a map that guides people on how to treat you. Marking paths that lead to mutual respect and understanding is more important than building walls.

Seek out relationships that are like a two-way street, where giving and receiving are in balance. Finding people that appreciate your empathy and respect your individuality is key. These relationships feel like a harmonious exchange, where both parties grow and thrive. Emotional independence is about recognizing that your emotional well-being is your own. It is understanding that while you can empathize with others, their emotions are not yours to fix. It is like being on a shared journey where you offer support but also honor your separate paths. Communicate openly and honestly. It is about expressing your feelings and needs without fear or hesitation. See every open conversation as a step toward a deeper, more authentic connection.

Finally, practice self-compassion. This is a journey about learning and growth, not about perfection. Every move you take, and every insight you gain, is a step toward happier, healthier relationships.

By embracing these changes, you are not just transforming your relationships; you are also rediscovering yourself. It is a journey that leads to a place where your empathy and your well-being coexist in beautiful harmony.

How to Build Healthy Independence

Building healthy independence is a unique process for you, especially after navigating the complexities of empathic and codependent tendencies. This journey is about crafting a life where your empathic abilities are an asset—not a liability—and where your sense of self is clear and strong.

Cultivating a Personal Philosophy: Develop a personal philosophy or mantra that resonates with your core values and beliefs. This philosophy should serve as a guiding principle in your life, helping you make decisions that align with your true self. It is like having a personal compass that keeps you oriented toward your authentic path.

Exploring New Horizons: Go out of your way to find challenges and new experiences that will take you outside of your comfort zone. This may be taking up a new hobby, visiting unfamiliar places, or trying out activities you have always wanted to do but have not yet. These experiences provide you with opportunities for personal growth and self-discovery by letting you discover facets of yourself that your relationships may have obscured.

Creating a Space for Self-Expression: Find a medium for self-expression that allows you to articulate your thoughts, feelings, and experiences. This could be through art, writing, music, or any form of creative expression. The act of creating something uniquely yours is a powerful affirmation of your individuality.

Nurturing Non-Romantic Relationships: Invest time and energy in nurturing non-romantic relationships that affirm your sense of self. Friendships and familial relationships can provide a supportive and grounding influence, reminding you of your worth and identity outside of romantic entanglements.

Practicing Mindful Solitude: Embrace periods of solitude mindfully. Use this time for introspection and self-care. Solitude can be a sanctuary where you reconnect with yourself, away from the influence and needs of others. It is not about isolation, but about cherishing moments of quiet self-reflection.

Realigning Life Goals: Take time to realign your life goals with your values and aspirations. In codependent relationships, it is common for personal aspirations to become entwined with those of others. Reclaiming and refocusing on your goals is a vital step in building your independent path.

Seeking Inspirational Role Models: Seek out mentors or role models who exhibit a healthy level of independence. These people can provide inspiration and practical insights on how to balance empathy with self-sufficiency. Learning from their experiences can offer valuable lessons that will help you pave your own path.

Building healthy independence is about creating a life where your empathic nature is celebrated and nurtured, but not at the expense of your growth and happiness. It is a journey toward a fulfilling life where your needs, dreams, and well-being are given the attention and respect they deserve.

Chapter 6:
The Myth of the Empathic Narcissist

Debunking the Myth About Empathic Narcissists

There is a paradox in the idea of an empathic narcissist, which has caused a lot of misunderstandings. Understanding the relationship between narcissism and empathy—and why true narcissists are incapable of displaying genuine empathy—is crucial to dispelling this misconception.

Narcissism, as defined in psychological terms, is characterized by traits such as grandiosity, a need for admiration, and a notable lack of empathy. Narcissists are often preoccupied with fantasies of success, power, or ideal love, and they may exploit relationships to serve their self-interest. At the core of narcissism is a fragile self-esteem, vulnerable to the slightest criticism. Empathy, on the other hand, is the ability to understand and share the feelings of others. It is a trait that entails emotional attunement, compassion, and the ability to place oneself in another person's shoes. Empathy is more than just cognitive understanding; it is an emotional connection and concern for the welfare of others.

The myth of the empathic narcissist likely stems from the narcissist's ability to mimic empathic behaviors. Incredibly charming and seemingly attentive, narcissists can give the impression of empathy. But frequently, this is just a surface-level show that is meant to manipulate and exert control. When a narcissist exhibits empathy, it is usually for their benefit, as opposed to genuine empathy, which is driven by a concern for others.

Understanding this distinction is crucial. The empathic behaviors exhibited by a narcissist are often strategic and aimed at gaining admiration, loyalty, or dependence. It is a facade that can be confusing and misleading, especially for those who are empathic themselves. The danger lies in mistaking this facade for true empathy, as it can lead to a misunderstanding of the narcissist's intentions and capabilities. Recognizing that a narcissist's empathy is often a tool rather than a genuine emotional connection is key to understanding and navigating relationships with such individuals.

Let us consider a real-life scenario to further clarify the idea of false empathy in narcissists. Take Daisy, for example, who was drawn to Robert because he was a charming and kind person. At first, Robert seemed to be the embodiment of compassion and understanding, always willing to lend a sympathetic ear. When they first started dating, Robert's attentiveness made Daisy feel seen and valued. He would often mirror her emotions, offering the right words of comfort and understanding. Daisy thought she had finally found someone who truly empathized with her feelings and needs. However, as their relationship developed, cracks began to show in Robert's empathic facade. Daisy noticed that Robert's displays of empathy were often tied to his needs and desires. When he was looking for admiration, support, or validation from her, that is when his attentiveness was most evident. His empathic demeanor would quickly fade when the focus shifted away from him. Daisy gradually came to see that Robert's empathy was conditioned and motivated by self-interest. Rather than being motivated by genuine concern, his ability to read her emotions was more about wanting to be in charge and be liked in the relationship. Robert was noticeably lacking in empathy when Daisy expressed needs or emotions that went against his plan. This realization was a game-changer for Daisy. She began to see that what she had perceived as empathy was a carefully crafted tool in Robert's narcissistic repertoire. His emotional attunement was a means to an end, lacking the depth and selflessness of true empathy.

Daisy's experience with Robert is a classic example of the myth of the empathic narcissist. It highlights how narcissists can skillfully mimic empathic behaviors, giving the impression of understanding and connection. This case highlights the significance of differentiating between genuine empathy and the strategic emotional displays that narcissists often exhibit. Understanding this distinction is crucial in navigating relationships with individuals who display narcissistic traits. Being aware of the telltale indicators of false empathy will shield you from emotional exploitation and manipulation and enable you to make informed decisions regarding your relationships.

Recognizing Narcissists Disguised as Empaths

Say you meet someone who seems to understand you like no one else ever has. They listen intently, their eyes lock onto yours, echoing every emotion you express. This person seems to embody the very essence of empathy. However, as time passes, you start noticing cracks in this perfect image. The once comforting gaze now feels like a performance, the understanding seems conditional, and the support wanes when it is not about them. This jarring realization makes you wonder: Was their empathy ever genuine?

This scenario is not unusual and can be unsettling. It serves as an acute reminder that not everyone who seems empathic is, in fact, such. Some people, especially those with narcissistic traits, are skilled at pretending to be empathic. What then distinguishes genuine empathy from a well-rehearsed act? Let us explore the signs that point to instances in which empathy is a facade for self-interest rather than a genuine understanding.

The Illusion of Instant Connection: Be mindful of people who create an immediate and intense sense of connection. While this can feel flattering and special, it is important to remember that deep, genuine connections usually develop over time. A narcissist might use this tactic to quickly gain your trust and affection.

Fluctuating Displays of Empathy: Notice if someone's empathic behavior comes and goes, especially in line with their personal goals or needs. Genuine empathy is consistent and not dependent on what someone can gain from the situation. If you observe empathy that seems to switch on and off, it might be a sign of a deeper, more self-serving motive.

Self-Centered Sensitivity: Take note of how frequently someone talks about their sensitivity or victimhood. While sharing personal experiences is normal, a narcissist may exaggerate their struggles in an attempt to gain sympathy or divert attention back to themselves.

Conditional Compassion: Genuine empathy is given freely and unconditionally. If you sense that someone's compassion or understanding is only present when it benefits them, it might be a red flag. True empathy does not come with strings attached.

Subtle Manipulation Through Empathy: Pay attention to how someone uses their understanding of your emotions. Does it feel like they are using this knowledge to control you, perhaps through guilt-tripping or gaslighting? These are manipulative tactics that a narcissist might disguise as empathy.

Lack of Depth in Emotional Connection: Reflect on the emotional depth of your interactions. Do they feel surface-level, despite the apparent empathy? Narcissists often struggle to form deep emotional bonds, which can leave relationships feeling somewhat hollow or one-sided.

Your Feelings After Interactions: After interacting with this person, pay attention to your feelings. Genuine empathic exchanges tend to be uplifting and comforting. If you are always drained, confused, or uneasy, it could indicate that the empathy you are receiving is not as genuine as it appears.

Overly Focused on Image and Perception: Notice if the person is excessively concerned about how others perceive them, especially in terms of being seen as empathic or caring. Narcissists often curate their image meticulously, and their display of empathy might be more about maintaining this image rather than genuine concern for others.

Rapid Shifts in Attitude: Be mindful of sudden changes in their attitude toward you or other people. A narcissist might be warm and understanding one moment and cold or dismissive the next, especially if their empathic behavior does not yield the expected results.

Empathy With an Audience: Look for signs of increased empathy when they are in public. In social settings or situations where there is a benefit to be gained from others seeing their compassionate side, narcissists frequently exhibit empathy more convincingly.

Lack of Follow-Through on Empathic Promises: Pay attention to whether their empathic expressions are followed by consistent actions. Even though they may say all the right things, narcissists often fail to follow through with genuinely empathic behavior.

Selective Empathy: Consider whether their empathy is selective, extended only to certain people, or in specific situations that benefit them. Genuine empathy is not typically selective but is a consistent trait applied across various relationships and circumstances.

Empathy Used as Leverage: Be cautious if it feels like their empathy is used as leverage or a bargaining tool in the relationship. If empathy is used to create a sense of debt or obligation, it is likely not coming from a place of genuine concern.

Discomfort With Genuine Emotional Sharing: Observe how they respond to genuine emotional sharing from your side. Narcissists often become uncomfortable or disinterested when the focus of empathy shifts away from them.

Now take a moment to reflect on your personal experiences. Ask yourself, "Have I ever felt a lingering doubt about the sincerity of someone's empathy, and how did it shape my trust and interaction with them?" This question is not just about identifying traits in others; it is about understanding your instincts and feelings and guiding you toward authentic and genuine connections.

Protecting Yourself From Narcissistic Deception

Reflecting on my encounters with narcissists posing as empaths, I realize the journey to understanding and protecting oneself is often filled with subtle revelations and hard-earned wisdom. Let me share a more nuanced aspect of my experience that might offer a fresh perspective.

During my interaction with Steve, a seemingly empathic individual, I initially found myself drawn in by what appeared to be genuine understanding and compassion. However, as our interactions deepened, I noticed moments where Steve's empathy seemed to be more about affirming his own identity as a caring person rather than truly understanding my feelings. It was a nuanced form of narcissism masquerading as empathy.

This experience taught me a lot, one of them is how crucial it is to differentiate between empathy that is offered and empathy that is sought. Genuine empathy is typically offered without a prompt, emanating naturally from the person's character. In contrast, Steve's empathy often seemed to require a cue or a setup, as if it were a response to a stage being set. Another subtle sign was the imbalance in emotional labor. True empathic connections are reciprocal; both parties share the emotional load. With Steve, I found myself consistently providing emotional support, with little genuine reciprocation. It was a one-sided emotional labor that left me drained, a classic hallmark of narcissistic relationships.

Observing the consistency of words and deeds is another skill I acquired. Narcissists can be adept at saying the right things, but their actions may tell a different story. In my case, Steve's actions often contradicted his empathic words, revealing a lack of genuine concern. I learned from this experience how important it is to pay attention to both what is being presented and what is missing in the interactions. Understanding the true nature of our relationship required recognizing the absence of genuine reciprocity, the need for emotional cues, and the incongruence between words and actions.

Navigating this path required me to develop a keen sense of observation and to trust my perceptions. It was a journey that went beyond the surface-level signs of empathy and delved into the subtler dynamics of emotional exchange. In sharing this experience, I hope to offer you insights that go beyond the conventional advice on dealing with narcissists. It is about developing a fine-tuned awareness of the emotional interplay in your relationships and trusting your ability to discern authenticity.

Setting Boundaries With Narcissists

Setting boundaries with narcissists, especially those who have mastered the art of feigning empathy, is a crucial skill for maintaining your emotional health and well-being. It is about drawing clear lines in your interactions, and ensuring that your needs and feelings are respected. Let me share a personal experience that highlights the significance of setting these boundaries and the impact it can have.

A few years ago, I encountered someone in my professional circle, whom I will call Jordan. Jordan had the charm and apparent empathy that initially made him seem like a supportive colleague. However, over time, I began to feel the strain of his overbearing presence and realized his empathy was often a tool for manipulation.

The first step in setting boundaries was recognizing the need for them. It became clear when I noticed how drained I felt after interactions with Jordan. His seemingly empathic concerns were often a prelude to requests for favors or support that were not reciprocated. I started by setting small, yet firm boundaries. This included saying "no" to unreasonable requests and being clear about my availability for work-related discussions. It was challenging at first, as Jordan did not respect these boundaries and often tried to guilt-trip me into compliance.

One of the most effective strategies was consistent enforcement of these boundaries. Each time Jordan attempted to overstep, I calmly but firmly reiterated my limits. It was not about confrontation but about asserting my right to a balanced professional relationship. Another crucial aspect was not to justify or over-explain my boundaries. Narcissists can use these explanations as loopholes to negotiate or argue. My boundaries were stated simply and clearly, leaving little room for misinterpretation. Over time, Jordan began to respect these boundaries, not out of understanding, but because it became clear that his usual tactics were no longer effective. This shift significantly improved my professional environment and reduced the emotional toll of our interactions.

This experience taught me that setting boundaries with narcissists is not only about protecting your time and energy but also about reclaiming your sense of self. It is a powerful affirmation of your worth and a statement that you are not susceptible to manipulative tactics. In sharing this, I aim to empower you with the understanding that while setting boundaries with narcissists can be challenging, it is both necessary and achievable. It is a crucial step in ensuring that your empathic nature is not exploited and that your interactions are healthy and respectful.

Empowering Yourself Against Narcissistic Manipulation

"Can you believe I fell for it again?" This was the question my friend Lara asked me one evening, her voice a mix of frustration and disbelief. She had just ended a relationship with someone she thought was deeply empathic, only to discover layers of manipulation beneath the compassionate facade. Her story is not unique; it is a narrative shared by many who have encountered narcissists skilled in the art of deception.

Lara's experience serves as a powerful reminder of the importance of empowering ourselves against narcissistic manipulation. It is about developing the tools and resilience to recognize and resist the sophisticated tactics employed by those who use empathy as a guise for control.

Recognizing the Patterns: Start by familiarizing yourself with the patterns of narcissistic manipulation. This knowledge is your shield. Narcissists often follow a predictable cycle of idealization, devaluation, and discard. Understanding this cycle can help you identify and respond to manipulation before it takes a toll.

Trust Your Intuition: Your intuition is a powerful ally. If something feels off in a relationship, pay attention to that feeling. Lara learned to trust her gut instincts, which often sensed inconsistencies and red flags long before her rational mind caught up.

Seek Objective Perspectives: Sometimes, our emotional involvement can cloud our judgment. Seeking objective perspectives from friends, family, or professionals can provide clarity. These external viewpoints can help validate your experiences and offer unbiased advice.

Practice Self-Advocacy: Empower yourself by practicing self-advocacy. This means expressing your needs and concerns clearly and assertively. Remember, your feelings and needs are valid, and advocating for them is a fundamental right.

Develop Emotional Boundaries: Setting and maintaining emotional boundaries is crucial. Determine what behaviors you are willing to accept and what crosses the line. Communicate these boundaries clearly, and be prepared to enforce them.

Cultivate a Support Network: Having a strong support network is invaluable. Surround yourself with people who uplift and support you. This network can provide emotional support, practical advice, and a sense of community.

Engage in Self-Care: Prioritize self-care. Engaging in activities that nurture your physical, emotional, and mental well-being can build resilience against manipulation. Self-care is an act of self-respect and a declaration of your worth.

Lara's journey, like that of many others, is a testament to the strength and resilience that can emerge in the face of narcissistic manipulation. By arming yourself with knowledge, trusting your intuition, and practicing self-care, you can empower yourself to navigate these challenging dynamics with confidence and clarity.

Chapter 7:
Facts About Narcissists That Empaths Should Know

The Truth About Narcissistic Exploitation

As difficult as it may be, empaths must understand the reality of narcissistic exploitation. Your emotional health may suffer greatly as a result of this exploitation, which is often subtle and insidious. Let us explore this reality, not to dishearten you, but to empower you with awareness and strategies for self-protection.

Take Emily's example, an empath who found herself in a relationship with Mark, a charismatic individual who appeared deeply understanding and caring at first. Emily, with her natural inclination to nurture, felt valued and heard in the early stages of their relationship. However, as time passed, the dynamics began to shift. Emily found herself increasingly drained, her own needs and feelings becoming secondary to Mark's. She was constantly catering to his demands, often feeling guilty for even considering her own well-being.

This scenario is a classic example of narcissistic exploitation. Narcissists, like Mark, are adept at spotting and taking advantage of the caring nature of empaths. They often present themselves as vulnerable and in need of support, tapping into the empath's innate desire to help. However, this vulnerability is often a facade—a means to an end. Exploitation can manifest in various forms—emotional, financial, or even physical. Narcissists may use guilt, flattery, or manipulation to keep empaths invested in the relationship. They create a cycle of dependency where the empath feels responsible for the narcissist's well-being, often at the cost of their own.

Understanding this reality is crucial. It involves spotting the signs of exploitation and understanding the dynamics at play. It is not about blaming yourself for being caring or empathic; it is about realizing that these qualities, while beautiful, can be misused by someone with narcissistic tendencies. The key to protecting yourself lies in recognizing the early signs of such exploitation. It involves setting boundaries, understanding your worth, and being mindful of the balance in your relationships. Remember, a healthy relationship is one where empathy and care are mutual, where your well-being is just as important as your partner's.

Empaths often find themselves in these challenging dynamics due to their compassionate nature. The empath's deep ability to feel and absorb the emotions of others can sometimes blur the lines of where their own needs begin and end. In relationships with narcissists, this can lead to a dangerous cycle of giving too much, receiving too little, and losing oneself in the process. The emotional toll of such relationships can be significant. You may find yourself feeling constantly anxious, depressed, or even physically unwell. The stress of trying to meet the endless needs of a narcissistic partner can drain your energy both emotionally and physically.

It is important to recognize that narcissistic exploitation is not just about overt abuse. It can also be about the gradual erosion of your sense of self, your boundaries, and your ability to prioritize your own needs. Narcissists often use subtle tactics like gaslighting, where they manipulate you into questioning your own reality and judgment. Confronting the reality of narcissistic exploitation is the first step in safeguarding yourself against it. It is a challenging truth, but one that empowers you to make informed decisions about your relationships and to protect your emotional health. By understanding these dynamics, you can begin to untangle yourself from the web of narcissistic exploitation and reclaim your sense of self.

Sometimes, the most profound insights come from introspection. As you consider your own experiences with narcissistic relationships, the questions below are intended to be gentle prompts, guiding you toward deeper self-awareness and understanding.

- Think about times when you have felt emotionally depleted after being with someone. What does this pattern tell you about the emotional give-and-take in your relationships?

- Recall instances where your kindness was seemingly taken for granted or used for someone else's gain. How did these experiences make you feel, and what did they teach you about your boundaries?

- Consider moments when you have found yourself making excuses for someone's lack of empathy or consideration. What drives you to justify these behaviors, and what might this suggest about the relationship's health?

- Reflect on any relationships where your needs seemed to become less important than your partner's. How has this imbalance affected your sense of self and emotional well-being?

- Ponder on relationships where feelings of obligation or guilt have overshadowed your own needs. Where do these feelings stem from, and how might they influence your choices and happiness?

- Think about how you respond to subtle manipulations like guilt-tripping or gaslighting. Are there ways you might better protect your emotional health in these situations?

- Consider the level of empathy you receive in your relationships. Does it feel like your empathic nature is genuinely appreciated and reciprocated?

These reflections are intended to guide you through a process of self-discovery and awareness. They are steps toward recognizing and addressing the challenges you may face in relationships with narcissists. By understanding your feelings and experiences, you can begin to take steps to protect your empathic nature and ensure your emotional needs are met.

Embracing the Unchangeable Nature of Narcissists

One of the most challenging truths for empaths to accept is the unchangeable nature of narcissists. This acceptance is not about condoning their behavior but about understanding a fundamental aspect of narcissism that can be crucial for your healing and growth. Let us delve into why recognizing and accepting this unchangeable nature is paramount.

Narcissism is deeply rooted in personality and often involves ingrained patterns of thinking and behavior that are resistant to change. Narcissists typically lack the self-awareness and willingness to change these patterns, as they do not see them as problematic. Instead, they often view their behavior as justified or a necessary part of who they are. For empaths, who are naturally inclined to see the good in others and believe in the potential for change, this can be a hard pill to swallow. You might find yourself holding onto hope that your love, understanding, and compassion can transform a narcissistic individual. However, this hope, while well-intentioned, can lead to a cycle of disappointment and emotional pain.

Accepting that a narcissist is unlikely to change requires a shift in perspective. It is about recognizing that your healing and well-being are not contingent on changing someone else. It is about redirecting your energy and empathy toward yourself and those who are capable of reciprocating your emotional investment. This acceptance does not mean you have to become cynical or lose your empathic nature. Instead, it is about applying your empathy wisely and protecting yourself from situations where it is likely to be exploited. It is about understanding that while everyone deserves compassion, not everyone will respond to it in the way you hope or expect.

Letting go of the need to change a narcissist can be liberating. It frees you from the burden of responsibility for their actions and behaviors. It allows you to focus on relationships that are healthier and more fulfilling, where your empathy is valued and returned.

Moving toward this acceptance involves a process of grieving. Grieving the loss of what you hoped the relationship could be, grieving the understanding that your love and care cannot heal every wound, and grieving the realization that some people will not change, no matter how much you want them to. In this grieving process, there is also growth. You learn to set healthier boundaries, value your own needs, and invest in relationships that bring mutual respect and fulfillment. This growth is a testament to your strength and resilience as an empath.

Accepting the unchangeable nature of narcissists is a crucial step in your journey. It is a step that leads to empowerment, self-care, and healthier relationships. It is a difficult but necessary part of embracing your empathic nature without sacrificing your well-being.

The Struggle of Empaths: Nurturing Hope Amid Harsh Realities

"Have you ever found yourself believing, against all odds, that your love could change someone?" This question lingered in my mind after a conversation with a friend, an empath, who had just ended a tumultuous relationship with a narcissist. She had clung to the hope that her compassion and understanding could bring about a change. It is a familiar narrative for many empaths; this unwavering belief in the transformative power of their love and empathy, even in the face of a harsher reality.

This dilemma—the empath's hope versus the stark reality of a narcissist's behavior—is a profound and often painful conflict. It challenges the very core of what many empaths believe: Deep understanding and unconditional love can heal and change anyone. But what if this belief, this beautiful and innate optimism, is more of a mirage when it comes to narcissists?

The truth can be uncomfortable and thought-provoking. Because they are so set in their ways, narcissists frequently exhibit little genuine desire to change. Their deeply ingrained personality traits dictate their behaviors, which are resistant to any empathic magic you may try to use. This insight may seem like a cold splash of reality after all of your fervent hopes and dreams. So, where does this leave you, the empath? You are at a crossroads where you must confront a challenging question: Are you holding onto hope at the expense of facing reality? This question is not meant to diminish the value of your empathy or your ability to love. Instead, it is an invitation to look at your relationships with clear eyes and perhaps a guarded heart.

Navigating this dilemma does not mean you have to lose your empathic nature or your hope for better, healthier relationships. Rather, it is about applying your empathy wisely, and understanding that while it is a gift, it is not a cure-all. It is about protecting your heart and your emotional well-being, even if it means accepting that some people, particularly narcissists, may not change, no matter how deeply you care.

This acceptance does not equate to cynicism; it is a form of emotional wisdom. It is recognizing that your empathy is precious and should be reserved for relationships where it is valued and reciprocated. It is about striking a balance between your hopeful nature and the reality of who you are dealing with. The empath's dilemma of hope versus reality is a journey of self-discovery. It is a path that asks you to reflect, to question, and to grow. It is about learning when to extend your empathy and when to protect it. This journey is challenging, but it is also a path to empowerment, self-respect, and ultimately, to more fulfilling and reciprocal relationships.

The Significance of Emotional Detachment

"Have you ever felt like you are losing yourself, piece by piece, in trying to hold onto someone else?" This question was posed to me by a friend over coffee, her eyes reflecting a mix of sadness and realization. She was an empath, deeply entangled in a relationship with a narcissist, and at a crossroads where the only path to self-preservation was emotional detachment. Her story, while unique in its details, is a familiar narrative for many empaths in similar situations. She described how her journey began with acknowledging the painful truth: Her emotional well-being was being eroded in the relentless cycle of trying to appease her narcissistic partner. The realization was not easy; it came with a heavy heart and a sense of mourning for the relationship she thought she had.

The first step in her path to detachment was recognizing her own needs and emotions as valid and important. For so long, she had placed her partner's needs above her own, often at the expense of her emotional health. She started to ask herself, "What do I need right now?" and "How do I feel about this?"—simple questions that slowly steered her toward reclaiming her emotional autonomy. Creating space was her next move, both physically and emotionally. She began to carve out time for herself, engaging in activities that she loved but had neglected. This space allowed her to reconnect with herself, to remember who she was outside the relationship.

Communicating her needs and boundaries became crucial. It was a challenging step, fraught with fear of conflict and guilt. But as she practiced expressing herself honestly and assertively, she found a new sense of empowerment. Each conversation was a step toward reaffirming her self-worth and establishing her emotional boundaries. Support from others was a lifeline during this time. Friends, family, and sometimes a therapist provided her with the strength and perspective she needed. They were her reminders that she was not alone and that her feelings were understood and shared by others.

Her journey of emotional detachment was not a linear path. There were moments of doubt; of slipping back into old patterns. But with each step forward, she grew stronger, more centered, and more in tune with her own needs and emotions. Her story is a powerful reminder of the importance of emotional detachment in relationships with narcissists. It is about finding the courage to prioritize your emotional well-being, recognize and honor your own needs, and step back from dynamics that drain your emotional energy. It is a journey that requires courage and self-compassion, but one that leads to a place of greater peace and self-respect.

Embarking on a New Chapter: Life Beyond Narcissistic Influence

Picture yourself at the brink of a new chapter in your life; the one where you emerge from the shadow of a narcissistic influence and find your own light. This is not just a dream; it is a possible and promising reality. Moving forward after the end of a relationship with a narcissist is more than just a process of recovery; it is a journey of rediscovery and empowerment.

First and foremost, acknowledge your strength. You have made it through a relationship that pushed the boundaries of your empathy and resilience. This alone demonstrates your inner strength, which you may now use to rebuild and redefine your life. Embrace the freedom that comes with this new chapter. You now have the opportunity to make choices that are entirely yours, free from the manipulation and control of a narcissistic partner. It is a chance to rediscover your passions, interests, and dreams. What were the things you loved doing that got sidelined? What are the places you want to explore? Now is the time to reconnect with those joys and aspirations.

Rebuilding your life also entails nurturing relationships that are healthy and reciprocal. Surround yourself with people who appreciate and respect your empathic nature; those who support and uplift you. These relationships, based on mutual respect and understanding, will be the cornerstone of your new life.

Invest in your personal growth. Whether it is through education, new hobbies, or personal development workshops, every step you take in learning and growing is a step toward a more fulfilling life. These experiences not only enrich your life but also strengthen your sense of self. Remember, healing is not a linear process. There will be days of doubt and setbacks, but these are not signs of failure. They are part of the human experience, and each one brings its own lessons and strengths. Be patient and kind to yourself as you navigate this journey. Most importantly, hold onto hope. The end of a relationship with a narcissist can be the beginning of something beautiful—a life where you are the author of your own story, where your empathy is a gift that enriches your life and the lives of others, and where your happiness is a reflection of your inner strength and wisdom.

Moving forward is not just about leaving something behind; it is about moving toward something wonderful—a life of self-discovery, growth, and true happiness. You have the power to create this life, and the journey starts now.

Chapter 8:
Setting and Maintaining Boundaries

Boundaries: Unlocking the Door to Genuine Relationships

"Remember the times when our conversations flowed endlessly without leaving us drained?" my friend pondered one evening. We were discussing how our interactions with others had evolved. For her, a self-identified empath, the journey toward setting boundaries had been transformative, especially in her relationships. This conversation sparked a realization: Boundaries, commonly perceived as obstacles, can serve as gateways to more genuine and fulfilling relationships.

For empaths, setting boundaries is more than just saying "no" or maintaining a distance; it involves creating a space where true connections can thrive. It is about articulating what you are comfortable with, how you wish to be treated, and your expectations from others. This clarity becomes the foundation for relationships to grow with mutual respect and understanding. The significance of boundaries in relationships is crucial, especially for empaths who often absorb the emotions and energies of those around them. Without boundaries, there is a risk of losing oneself in the needs and desires of others, leading to emotional exhaustion and a loss of personal identity. Boundaries play a vital role in preserving emotional energy and ensuring that relationships are mutually nurturing.

So, how do boundaries contribute to authenticity in relationships? It begins with the understanding that setting boundaries means being true to oneself and honoring one's needs, values, and feelings. This honesty creates a template for others to understand and respect the core of who you are, inviting genuine interactions with your true self, free from overextension or compromise. Setting boundaries also signifies a level of self-awareness and self-acceptance that is deeply attractive. It demonstrates that you value yourself and are confident in your skin, setting the stage for relationships based on genuine respect and admiration. Moreover, setting boundaries permits others to do the same, fostering a healthier dynamic where both parties feel safe expressing their needs and limits. This promotes communication and understanding essential for any strong relationship.

Certainly, setting boundaries is not always easy, particularly for empaths who may fear that it will push others away or make them seem uncaring. However, the opposite is often true. Boundaries can strengthen relationships by preventing resentment, misunderstanding, and burnout, allowing you to give freely and wholeheartedly from a place of self-care, not obligation. Boundaries are not merely protective walls; they serve as bridges connecting you to others in a more meaningful and authentic way. They enable you to interact with the world while staying true to yourself, inviting others to meet you at a level of honesty and respect. For empaths, mastering the art of setting boundaries is a crucial step toward building and maintaining relationships that are deeply rewarding and genuinely fulfilling.

Consider these questions to deepen your understanding and application of this idea in your own life:

- Reflect on your current boundaries. Are they clear, flexible, or perhaps non-existent? How do these boundaries reflect your values and needs?

- Consider your emotions in relationships where boundaries are respected versus those where they are not. What does this tell you about the importance of boundaries in your relationships?

- Recall a time when setting a boundary improved a relationship. What did it teach you about the role of boundaries in enhancing mutual respect and understanding?

- Identify fears or challenges holding you back from setting firm boundaries. How can you overcome these obstacles to establish healthier boundaries?

- Evaluate your approach to communicating boundaries. Is it clear and assertive, or do you find it difficult to articulate your limits?

- Explore practical steps to improve the clarity and effectiveness of your boundaries, such as being more assertive, reevaluating your limits, or seeking support from others.

- Reflect on your reactions when someone challenges or disrespects your boundaries. Are there more effective ways to respond to protect your emotional well-being?

The Art of Saying "No"

One evening, a friend shared a story that resonated deeply with me. She recounted a moment when she courageously uttered the word "no" to a demanding acquaintance. As she spoke, the palpable fear and uncertainty were evident, yet so was the profound sense of liberation that enveloped her afterward. This experience marked a pivotal shift in her life—a stride toward greater self-empowerment and self-respect. Her story is a poignant illustration of the complex yet rewarding journey of learning to say "no" for those who naturally lean toward saying "yes."

For many, the act of saying "no" is fraught with internal conflict. The innate desire to help, to heal, and to be there for others often comes into conflict with the need for self-care and personal boundaries. Yet, within the simple word "no" lies a latent strength. It transcends mere refusal; it stands as a proclamation of self-worth, a demarcation of personal space, and an indispensable element in maintaining a harmonious equilibrium between one's needs and those of others.

The empowerment derived from uttering "no" cannot be overstated. It signifies the realization that your time and energy hold value and that you possess the autonomy to decide how to allocate these precious resources. It involves understanding that, at times, saying "no" to someone else is, in essence, saying "yes" to your own well-being.

The journey toward comfortably expressing "no" commences with the recognition of your boundaries. What situations leave you feeling depleted or resentful? Identifying these scenarios serves as the initial stride in discerning where you need to draw the line. Conveying your "no" presents the subsequent challenge. It entails clarity, directness, and, most crucially, compassion toward yourself. It is imperative to bear in mind that you are not accountable for others' reactions to your boundaries. Your responsibility lies in communicating your needs in a considerate and truthful manner.

This journey is not devoid of challenges. You might encounter resistance, feel guilty, or fear the loss of relationships. However, each time you assert your "no," you reinforce your boundaries, affirm your self-worth, and take control of your emotional health. As you embrace the practice of saying "no," you will notice a transformation in your life. Relationships become more authentic, your time more rewarding, and your sense of self more solid. In the space created by your boundaries, there is room for growth, peace, and meaningful connections.

Mastering the art of saying "no" is a vital skill, transforming a perceived vulnerability into a source of strength. It is a journey that leads to a more empowered, balanced, and fulfilling existence.

Boundaries in Digital Spaces

In the digital era, empaths come to a subtle yet profound realization: The screens before us, teeming with a continuous flow of information and emotion, are more than mere windows to the world—they are reflective mirrors of our own emotional states. For empaths, who traverse the world with heightened emotional awareness, the digital realm poses a distinctive array of challenges and opportunities. It is a space where boundaries are not just beneficial but vital for preserving emotional well-being and maintaining clarity.

The digital domain remains an unexplored terrain for many empaths. It is a realm where emotions are intensified, and where the joy and pain of multitudes can be encountered in a few scrolls. This constant exposure to a broad spectrum of emotions can be overwhelming, akin to navigating a bustling city and absorbing the mood, thoughts, and energy of every passerby. Without a map or a set of guidelines, it is easy to become lost in this digital metropolis.

For empaths, successfully navigating this space hinges on the establishment of firm, clear boundaries. These boundaries are not walls to shut out the world; instead, they act as filters, enabling a more selective and intentional engagement with the digital world.

The journey commences with self-awareness. Recognizing what impacts you most in the digital realm is crucial. Is it anxiety-inducing news? Draining posts from specific friends? The feeling of obligation to respond to every comment or message? Identifying these triggers marks the initial stride toward cultivating a healthier digital environment. Once triggers are identified, the next step involves curating your digital experience. This entails being discerning about who and what you permit into your digital space. Follow accounts that inspire and uplift, and set boundaries around content that tends to deplete your energy. Your social media feed is your space, and you wield the power to shape it.

Effective time management is another critical facet of digital boundaries. Social media platforms are designed to encourage endless scrolling, leading to unplanned and unproductive hours. By allocating specific times for social media use, you regain control over your time and, more importantly, your energy. This disciplined approach prevents the sensation of being adrift in the digital cacophony. Mindful engagement is equally crucial. Before reacting to a post or comment, pause and check in with yourself. Ask, "Is this interaction in alignment with my emotional well-being?" If the answer is "no," allow yourself to step back. Not every digital interaction merits your emotional investment. Finally, consider integrating regular digital detoxes into your routine. These breaks offer opportunities to disconnect from the digital world and reconnect with yourself and your immediate surroundings. Utilize this time for activities that rejuvenate your energy and bring joy.

Through the establishment of these boundaries, the digital world transforms into a realm of empowerment rather than overwhelm. It becomes a space where you can connect, learn, and grow—on your terms and in ways that honor your emotional needs and boundaries.

As an empath, your profound capacity to feel is a formidable gift. In the digital age, where emotions are as prevalent as the information they accompany, setting boundaries is not just a strategy; it is an act of self-care. It ensures that your engagement with the digital world is balanced, healthy, and aligned with your emotional landscape.

Trusting Your Intuition

Have you ever experienced a subtle inner nudge or a soft, internal voice that seems to guide you in moments of uncertainty? This is your intuition, a remarkable yet often underestimated facet of your consciousness. For empaths, intuition is not merely a whisper; it is a potent tool, an internal compass that steers them through the intricate emotional landscapes they navigate daily.

At its core, intuition is intricately linked to the concept of boundaries. It acts as a protector, signaling when something feels amiss or when a situation might be potentially harmful. For empaths, whose sensitivity to emotions is heightened, recognizing and trusting these intuitive signals is paramount. It is akin to possessing an internal alarm system that notifies you when your boundaries are being tested or breached.

One of the biggest challenges empaths encounter is the conflict between their intuitive feelings and the demands of the external world. Society often places a premium on logic over feelings, leading many to dismiss their gut instincts. However, for an empath, neglecting these intuitive cues can result in emotional overload and distress. Trusting your intuition entails honoring your feelings, even when they diverge from societal expectations.

The journey to trust your intuition is a gradual process. It commences with acknowledging its existence and understanding its value in your life. Reflect on instances when your intuition guided you correctly and consider moments when disregarding it led to discomfort or pain. These diverse experiences all serve as lessons in the art of listening to your inner voice. Intuition plays a pivotal role in setting and maintaining boundaries. It often manifests as a sensation—a feeling of discomfort, unease, or conversely, a sense of peace and alignment. By attuning themselves to these feelings, empaths can gain a better understanding of where to draw the line in relationships, work, and social interactions. It is not about building walls; rather, it is about recognizing the boundaries of your emotional space.

Celebrating Victories in Boundary Setting

As you embark on this journey of self-discovery and empowerment, it is essential to pause and recognize the victories you achieve along the way. These moments, no matter how small they may seem, are significant milestones in your path toward a more balanced and fulfilling life.

Think about the last time you set a boundary and held onto it, despite the challenges. Maybe you said no to an extra task at work that would have overwhelmed your schedule, or perhaps you chose to spend a quiet evening alone instead of attending a social event that did not align with your current state of mind. These instances, these choices, are your victories. They are powerful affirmations of your self-worth and your commitment to taking care of yourself. Recognizing these victories extends beyond a simple pat on the back; it is about reinforcing the positive changes you are instigating in your life. Every time you acknowledge a successfully set boundary, you fortify your commitment to maintaining these healthy limits in the future. It is akin to building muscle; the more you appreciate your ability to set boundaries, the stronger and more confident you become in doing so.

Now, let us explore ways to celebrate these wins. Celebration need not always be extravagant; it is about acknowledging your progress in a manner that resonates with you. Consider documenting your achievements in a journal, reflecting on the emotions these moments elicited and the positive impact they have had on your life. Alternatively, share your successes with a supportive friend who understands your journey. Sometimes, vocalizing your victories can amplify their significance. Another impactful way to celebrate is by indulging in self-treatment. This might involve savoring a favorite cup of tea, taking a stroll in nature, or engaging in a hobby that brings you joy. These acts of self-care are more than just rewards; they serve as reminders that your needs and happiness hold importance.

As you progress along this path, remember that every small step forward contributes to your growth. There may be occasions when setting boundaries feels challenging, and that is perfectly okay. The key is that you are making an effort, learning, and, most importantly, evolving. Embrace these small victories as the fuel propelling you forward and the guiding light on your journey toward a more empathic and balanced life. Your ability to set and celebrate boundaries is not just a skill; it is a gift you bestow upon yourself—a testament to your strength and your dedication to living a life that authentically reflects who you are.

A Shared Path to Understanding

As we navigate through the complexities of relationships and self-discovery, there is a unique opportunity that extends beyond just reading these pages. Your journey, filled with personal insights and reflections, is a vital part of a larger narrative. Consider the moments of realization, the echoes of your experiences, and the insights you have gained. This is not just about absorbing information; it is about engaging in a conversation that extends beyond the individual. Your perspective is a valuable part of this ongoing dialogue.

By sharing your honest and genuine review, you contribute more than just feedback; you offer guidance and solidarity to others on similar paths. Your thoughts and reflections can be a beacon for someone else seeking understanding and validation in their own experiences with complex relationships. Imagine the impact of your words on someone who is seeking validation or a new perspective. Your review could be the encouragement they need to explore these concepts further and find solace or understanding in their situation.

Leaving a review is an act of participation in a broader conversation. It is about adding your voice to a community that values understanding, support, and collective wisdom. Every review, whether it resonates with positivity or offers constructive critique, enriches this conversation, contributing to a diverse and inclusive understanding. As you continue your journey through these pages, I invite you to reflect on the idea of sharing your experience. Think about how your unique journey, with its challenges and victories, could resonate with someone else in the community of readers.

Your review is more than just words; it is an extension of your journey, a contribution to a collective narrative of learning and healing. Your voice is important, and I eagerly anticipate your honest reflections. Thank you for being a part of this shared path. Your time, openness, and willingness to share are deeply appreciated. Together, we are not just individuals on separate journeys; we are a community united in our quest for deeper understanding and growth.

With gratitude, Rachel

Scan to leave a review on
Amazon if you live in the US

Scan to leave a review on
Amazon if you live in the UK

Scan to leave a review on
Amazon if you live in Canada

Scan to leave a review on
Amazon if you live in Australia

Chapter 9:
Empowering the Empath

Unlocking Personal Growth Through Empathic Abilities

T ake a moment to reflect on instances when your empathy felt like a double-edged sword—a gift that allowed you to connect deeply with others, yet sometimes left you feeling overwhelmed and drained. What if I told you that this very gift, which has been both your strength and vulnerability, holds the key to unlocking new dimensions of personal growth for you? Visualize channeling this profound sensitivity beyond navigation, into innovation. Your empathic abilities can catalyze creative problem-solving and ideation. Consider how your intuitive grasp of emotions might lead to insights others overlook. What unique solutions could you generate, solutions resonating on a deeply human level?

Now, reconsider the concept of leadership. While tradition may associate leadership with authority, empathy has the power to redefine it. As an empath, your capacity to connect, understand, and inspire transcends the conventional. How might your empathic nature reshape your approach to leading, influencing, and motivating those around you?

Explore the art of emotional alchemy. You have likely mastered managing the emotions you absorb, but what about transforming these emotions into positive, empowering energy? This goes beyond coping; it involves actively using these emotions to fuel creativity, propel ambitions, and deepen self-understanding.

In decision-making, delve into strategic empathy. Balancing empathy with rational thought can yield more holistic and effective decisions. Ponder how combining empathic insights with logical analysis could lead to decisions that are both impactful and considerate of all involved. Consider the depth of your intuitive understanding, a product of empathy. This intuition can serve as a guiding light in your journey. How can you further attune to this intuition, allowing it to illuminate your path, anticipate challenges, and seize opportunities?

Lastly, recognize the power of empathic communication in conflict resolution. Your natural ability to perceive and articulate emotions is a potent tool for finding common ground and understanding. How can you leverage this skill to not merely navigate but resolve conflicts, turning tense moments into opportunities for connection and understanding?

As you contemplate these possibilities, remember that your journey as an empath is unique and ever-evolving. Each step opens new doors, offering opportunities to transform not only how you interact with the world but also how you understand and grow within yourself. Your empathic nature is not merely a facet of you; it is a compass guiding you toward deeper, more meaningful personal growth.

The Power of Emotional Intelligence

In a quaint coffee shop nestled within the heart of a bustling city, a young woman named Sophie sat, navigating the ebb and flow of emotions around her. As an empath, Sophie had often grappled with the overwhelming nature of the feelings she absorbed. However, on a particularly challenging day, amid the swirl of emotions, she had an epiphany. What she once perceived as a burden was, in fact, a unique gift—an emotional intelligence that held the key to a deeper understanding of herself and those around her. This realization marked the beginning of Sophie's journey toward harnessing her emotional intelligence for personal empowerment.

Much like Sophie, you may have encountered moments where your empathic nature felt more like a challenge than a gift. Yet, have you considered that this sensitivity could be the very force that empowers you in various aspects of your life? Emotional intelligence, the ability to perceive, understand, and manage emotions, is a skill inherent to empaths. It has the transformative potential not only to shape your self-perception but also to redefine your interactions with the world.

Envision yourself as a skilled navigator, gracefully steering through the intricate seas of human emotion. This is the potential unlocked by developing your emotional intelligence. It goes beyond merely sensing emotions; it involves interpreting them, understanding their origins, and using this insight to cultivate deeper connections, make informed decisions, and lead a more fulfilling life.

Consider the instances when you sensed a friend's unspoken sadness or a colleague's concealed frustration. This intuitive understanding is a powerful tool at your disposal. Yet, it is not solely about understanding others; it is equally about comprehending yourself. Reflecting on the origins of your own emotions and what they communicate is a vital aspect of developing emotional intelligence. Furthermore, emotional intelligence emphasizes balance. It encompasses not only empathizing with others but also maintaining your emotional equilibrium. As an empath, you may find yourself absorbing too much, leading to emotional fatigue. Learning to regulate these emotions, distinguishing between what is yours and what belongs to others, is crucial for sustaining your emotional well-being.

Now, envision employing this emotional intelligence in conflict resolution or problem-solving. Your ability to comprehend and articulate emotions can transform challenging situations into opportunities for growth and connection. It involves finding harmony amid discord and understanding within misunderstanding. As you embark on the journey of cultivating your emotional intelligence, remember that it is an ongoing process. Embrace your empathic nature and utilize it to empower not only yourself but also those around you. Your empathy is a gift—a tool for deeper understanding and connection. It is time to celebrate and fully embrace this facet of yourself, recognizing it as the unique and valuable trait it is.

Building Emotional Resilience

In the quiet embrace of an autumn evening, bathed in the whispers of rustling leaves, I sat in the subdued glow of my living room, deep in contemplation. It was a moment of serene introspection following a day that had tested the bounds of my empathic nature. As an empath, the emotions of others had always coursed through me intensely, as if they were my own. On that particular day, the emotional currents from those around me had surged to a point where I felt inundated—a vessel on the verge of overflow.

In that profound moment, I recognized the imperative need to cultivate resilience, not merely as a shield but as a skill. It became clear that resilience was not a barricade to hide behind; rather, it was a mastery, a tool to navigate the tumultuous emotional tides without losing oneself within them.

A crucial lesson in my resilience journey was the art of emotional separation. Amid a challenging family gathering, conflicting emotions swirled around me, each vying for acknowledgment. It was overwhelming. Yet, amid the chaos, I discovered the ability to discern my feelings from those surrounding me. I envisioned an ethereal barrier—a gentle yet unyielding boundary that separated my emotional space from theirs. It was a revelation, realizing I could empathize without shouldering everyone else's emotional burdens as my own.

Emotional alchemy emerged as another pivotal step in my resilience journey. During a moment of profound personal low, burdened by a friend's distress I had unintentionally internalized, I chose to transmute this emotional weight into creativity. Turning to my canvas and paints, each brushstroke became a release—a transformation of empathy into art. This experience revealed that emotions, even the overwhelming ones, could be channeled into something beautiful and healing.

Engaging in mindful self-reflection became a daily ritual. Each evening, I retreated to quiet solitude, contemplating the day's emotions—both mine and those absorbed from others. This practice fostered a profound understanding of my emotional patterns and triggers, akin to rediscovering the depths of my own heart.

The most profound lesson in resilience was embracing the power of vulnerability. Initially perceived as a fragile aspect requiring protection, my empathic nature took on a new light when I realized that vulnerability was not weakness—it was strength. It enabled me to connect authentically with others on a profound level. Embracing vulnerability became a journey of acceptance, understanding that being an empath was not about shielding oneself from the world but authentically engaging with it, heart fully invested.

One particularly effective strategy in this journey is the Visualization Shield exercise. More than a coping mechanism, it becomes a method to navigate life's emotional complexities with empowerment and clarity.

Envision standing on the precipice of an emotionally charged scenario, whether a family event or a demanding workday. Before entering, engage in the Visualization Shield exercise—a practice preparing you to interact with the world in a balanced, healthy manner. Find a quiet space, creating a mental sanctuary for the exercise. Close your eyes, focusing on your breath, allowing each inhale to deepen your calm. In your mind's eye, visualize a protective shield forming around you—a bubble of light, an energetic cloak, or a transparent dome. Choose an image evoking safety and protection. This shield is your personal barrier, a filter between you and the emotional energies around you. Visualize the shield as selectively permeable, allowing positive experiences to pass through while acting as a barrier against negative energies. Affirm to yourself, "I am aware of the emotions around me, but I remain centered within my shield. It protects me and allows me to choose how I interact with these emotions." As you feel the shield firmly in place, return your awareness to your surroundings. Open your eyes, carrying the sense of safety and emotional autonomy that your shield provides. After emotionally charged encounters, reflect on the experience. How did the shield impact your ability to manage emotions? How did you feel during and after? Reflecting on these questions enhances your practice over time.

Integrating the Visualization Shield exercise into your routine can significantly transform how you navigate emotional landscapes. With practice, it becomes a natural aspect of your approach to emotional resilience, enabling empathic engagement while safeguarding your emotional well-being.

Thriving in Personal and Professional Life

As we delve deeper into the empath's journey, a pivotal aspect emerges—thriving in both personal and professional realms. For empaths, this transcends conventional success; it is about flourishing while staying authentic to their empathic nature.

In personal relationships, being an empath brings both profound rewards and challenges. The ability to deeply connect emotionally enhances relationships, yet the risk of absorbing others' emotions looms large. Thriving involves striking a balance between empathy and self-care. Recognizing when to offer support and when to retreat for emotional replenishment is key—understanding that caring for others should not eclipse one's own needs.

In the professional sphere, empaths possess unique skills that can be invaluable. Sensing emotional nuances, empathizing with colleagues, and anticipating needs make empaths exceptional team players or leaders. However, the challenge lies in preventing emotional burnout. Thriving at work involves setting clear emotional boundaries and seeking roles that align with empathic strengths—positions involving teamwork, creativity, or helping others. Effectively communicating needs is crucial in the workplace. Open discussions about the work environment, such as the need for a quiet space or task flexibility, help harness empathic abilities without depleting them.

Embracing and owning one's empathic nature is vital. Being an empath is a strength to celebrate—a unique ability to connect deeply and empathize. This celebration is not just self-acceptance; it is empowerment, inspiring both oneself and others.

Let us explore some practical real-life scenarios. These scenarios are designed to help you navigate common situations you might encounter, offering strategies and resolutions that honor your empathic nature.

Scenario 1: Overwhelmed at a Family Gathering

Imagine you are at a family gathering, and the house is buzzing with a mix of emotions—excitement, stress, joy, and perhaps some underlying tensions. As an empath, you start to feel overwhelmed, absorbing all these emotions until they become your own.

Resolution:

- Step away for a moment to a quiet space, like a garden or an unoccupied room.

- Take deep breaths and visualize your emotional shield, separating your feelings from those around you.

- Return to the gathering with a renewed sense of calm, engaging in conversations at your own pace and intensity.

Scenario 2: High-Pressure Meeting at Work

You are in a high-pressure meeting at work, with tight deadlines and high stakes. The stress and anxiety in the room are palpable, and you find yourself absorbing these emotions, feeling increasingly anxious.

Resolution:

- Ground yourself by focusing on physical sensations, like the feel of your feet on the floor or the texture of the table.

- Maintain a mental note that these emotions are not yours; you are sensing the room's atmosphere.

- After the meeting, take a short walk or find a quiet spot to decompress and release any absorbed stress.

Scenario 3: Supporting a Friend in Distress

A close friend is going through a tough time and turns to you for support. You listen and empathize deeply, but afterward, you feel emotionally drained, carrying the weight of your friend's problems.

Resolution:

- After your conversation, engage in a self-care activity that you enjoy, like reading, listening to music, or a hobby.

- Reflect on the interaction, acknowledging your feelings and reminding yourself that while you care for your friend, their problems are not yours to solve.

- If needed, gently communicate your boundaries to your friends, letting them know you are there for them but also need to take care of your own emotional well-being.

Scenario 4: Navigating Office Politics

In your workplace, you find yourself caught in the middle of office politics. You can sense the underlying tensions and unspoken conflicts, which start to affect your mood and productivity.

Resolution:

- Choose to engage selectively in conversations, focusing on work-related discussions and steering clear of gossip or conflict-laden topics.

- Use your empathic abilities to understand different perspectives, but remain neutral and avoid taking sides.

- If the environment becomes too toxic, consider discussing your concerns with a supervisor or exploring other roles within the organization that might be better suited to your empathic nature.

These scenarios highlight the importance of understanding your empathic limits and employing strategies to navigate challenging situations effectively. By acknowledging your emotional responses and taking proactive steps to manage them, you can maintain your well-being while still engaging deeply and meaningfully with the world around you.

Celebrating and Embracing Your Empathic Superpower

Have you ever felt like a chameleon, constantly changing colors to match the emotional landscapes of those around you? This feeling might resonate deeply if you are an empath. It is a shared experience, where your own emotions seem to mirror the joys and sorrows of the world. But what if this chameleon-like ability is not just a survival tactic, but a genuine superpower?

Let us embark on a journey of self-discovery and empowerment, turning the lens inward to explore the depths of your empathic nature. It is a less-traveled path, often misunderstood, yet incredibly rewarding.

Firstly, let us address a common fear which is the overwhelming nature of being an empath. While it can be daunting to feel the world so deeply, consider this—your sensitivity is a beacon in a sometimes dark world. It makes you an extraordinary listener, a trusted confidant, and a deeply compassionate friend. These are not just qualities; they are gifts. Now, imagine owning your empathic nature as embracing a secret inner strength. It is about acknowledging that your ability to feel deeply is not a burden, but a powerful tool for navigating the complexities of human relationships. This realization is both liberating and empowering.

But how do you celebrate this part of yourself? It starts with self-acceptance. Embrace your empathy with the same compassion you offer others. Recognize that your emotional depth is a source of wisdom and insight. Use this insight to guide others—whether through mentoring, counseling or simply being there for someone in need. Your empathic abilities can be a guiding light for those lost in their own emotional darkness.

In your professional life, this empathic nature can be your greatest asset. Imagine understanding your colleagues and clients on a deeper level, anticipating needs, and responding with empathy. This ability can transform your workplace relationships, creating a harmonious and productive environment.

However, even the strongest empaths need to recharge. It is essential to create boundaries and find time for self-care. Whether through meditation, nature walks, or creative pursuits, find what rejuvenates your spirit and allows you to reconnect with your inner self.

In conclusion, your empathic nature is a gift to be celebrated—a unique lens through which you experience the world. By owning and embracing it, you open yourself up to a life of deeper connections, personal growth, and an unparalleled ability to positively impact the lives of others. So, stand tall in your empathy, and let it be your guiding light.

Chapter 10:
Developing Empathic Wisdom

Fostering Intuition and Inner Guidance

P icture yourself traversing a dense forest, uncertainty shrouding the path ahead. Suddenly, a gentle inner voice whispers, guiding you toward a clearing. This mirrors the empath's odyssey, navigating life's intricacies guided by the subtle yet potent voice of intuition. For empaths, intuition transcends mere hunches; it evolves into profound inner wisdom that serves as an invaluable compass amid life's overwhelming emotions. So, how does one nurture and cultivate this inner guidance? The journey commences with trust—trust in the quiet nudges and gentle murmurs emanating from the depths of your heart.

The initial step in this cultivation involves creating a sanctuary for silence and contemplation. Amid the clamor of daily life, an empath's sensitive radar can be inundated with external stimuli. Hence, finding moments of solitude becomes essential. Be it through meditation, a serene walk in nature, or merely sitting in quiet reflection, these interludes of stillness allow you to authentically connect with your inner voice. Yet, cultivating intuition is not solely about discovering quietude; it is also about actively listening and acknowledging what you hear. Empaths may grapple with self-doubt, particularly when their sentiments and perceptions diverge from the rational world. It is paramount to honor your feelings and the insights originating from within, even when they defy conventional logic. Your intuition amalgamates emotional intelligence, life experiences, and empathic sensitivity—deserving recognition.

Another pivotal facet is practice. Similar to any skill, intuition sharpens with consistent practice. Initiate with minor decisions, tuning into your feelings about each option. Pay attention to the sensations in your body—the gut feelings, the heart's murmurs. Do you sense ease or discomfort? These bodily cues often constitute the language of your intuition.

Journaling stands as a potent tool in this journey. By documenting your experiences, emotions, and inner guidance, you forge a tangible record of your intuitive process. Over time, discerning patterns and comprehending how your intuition communicates with you becomes feasible. This self-awareness represents a crucial stride in trusting and fortifying your inner guidance.

Lastly, distinguishing between fear and intuition assumes significance. Fear typically manifests as loud, urgent, and rooted in past insecurities or traumas. In contrast, intuition is gentle, reassuring, and grounded in the present moment. Acquiring the ability to differentiate between these two empowers you to trust and depend on your intuition more assuredly.

In conclusion, cultivating intuition entails a journey of trust, practice, and self-awareness. It encompasses creating a receptive space to listen, honoring what you hear, and learning to discriminate between fear and authentic inner guidance. As you embark on this journey, bear in mind that your intuition is a distinctive gift—a guiding light that illuminates your path with wisdom and insight.

Learning From Emotional Signals

Imagine emotions as a spectrum of colors, each hue representing a different feeling. For empaths, this spectrum is vivid and intense, with each color telling its own story. Learning from these emotional signals is like becoming an artist who understands the deeper meanings behind each shade and stroke.

The first step in this artistic journey is to cultivate a keen awareness of your emotional palette. As an empath, you encounter a diverse array of emotions, both yours and those of others. Rather than succumbing to the intensity, approach it with curiosity. Each emotion, whether it is the deep blue of sadness or the fiery red of anger, carries a message about your inner world and the surrounding environment. Imagine a scenario where frustration surges suddenly. Instead of reacting impulsively, pause and delve into this emotion.

What is the source of this frustration? Is it a reflection of something within you, or are you tuning into someone else's frustrations? This exploration can lead to valuable insights, aiding you in navigating your emotional landscape with greater clarity.

Emotions are intricately connected with physical sensations. Paying attention to how your body responds to different emotions provides clues about their origins and meanings. A knot in your stomach during anxiety or a sense of lightness in joy—tuning into these bodily responses enhances your understanding of emotional signals.

Embrace the entire spectrum of emotions. Society often labels emotions as positive or negative, but each emotion serves a purpose and holds value. Anger can instigate change, sadness can foster empathy, and even fear can be a source of motivation. Accept and explore each emotion without judgment to learn from them. Sharing your emotional experiences with others can be enlightening. Engaging in heartfelt conversations with friends, family, or support groups offers fresh perspectives and insights into your emotional experiences. These discussions broaden your understanding of emotions, placing them in a larger context.

Remember that learning from emotional signals is an ongoing process requiring patience, self-compassion, and a willingness to embrace the complexity of your emotional world. As you continue to explore and understand your emotions, they become less overwhelming and more informative, guiding you toward greater self-awareness and emotional wisdom. Emotions are not merely fleeting feelings; they are guides, teachers, and storytellers. By approaching them with awareness, curiosity, and openness, you can transform your emotional experiences into a source of wisdom and insight, enriching both your personal growth and your ability to connect with others.

Here are some thought-provoking questions to guide you in this journey of emotional exploration:

- When you feel a strong emotion, ask yourself, "Is this feeling originating from within me, or am I absorbing it from my surroundings?" This question helps in distinguishing between personal emotions and those empathically absorbed from others.

- Every emotion carries a message. When you experience a particular feeling, especially a strong or recurring one, ask, "What is this emotion trying to tell me about my needs, boundaries, or values?" This reflection can reveal underlying personal truths or areas needing attention.

- Consider how your body reacts to different emotions. Ask yourself, "Where do I feel this emotion in my body, and what is this physical sensation telling me?" This question can help you connect emotional experiences with physical responses, deepening your self-awareness.

- Reflect on the context in which the emotion arises. "What situations, people, or environments trigger this emotion?" Understanding the context can provide insights into your emotional triggers and how to manage them.

- Look for patterns in your emotional responses. "Are there specific times, situations, or people that consistently evoke certain emotions in me?" Recognizing patterns can be key to understanding deeper emotional habits and tendencies.

- When you feel an intense emotion, pause and ask, "Am I reacting impulsively to this emotion, or can I respond to it in a more thoughtful, measured way?" This question encourages you to take a step back and choose responses that align with your values and well-being.

- After sharing your emotions with someone, reflect on the interaction. "What did I learn about my emotions from this conversation? Did the perspective of others offer me new insights?" This can help you see your emotional experiences through a different lens.

- When you find yourself labeling an emotion as "good" or "bad," ask, "What can I learn from this emotion, regardless of its nature?" This encourages you to find value and lessons in every emotional experience.

- Ask yourself, "How have my emotional experiences contributed to my growth? What changes can I make to better manage and learn from my emotions?" This reflection can guide you toward personal development and emotional wisdom.

By regularly engaging with these questions, you can deepen your understanding of your emotional signals. This process is not just about managing emotions but about transforming them into a source of wisdom and insight, enriching your journey as an empath.

Gaining Insights From Past Relationships

Reflecting on past relationships can be like looking through a rearview mirror; it offers clarity and perspective on the road traveled, helping us navigate future paths with greater wisdom. For empaths, this reflection is not just about understanding what happened, but also about gaining insights into their own emotional patterns and tendencies.

The empath's journey in relationships is often intense and deeply felt. You may have experienced relationships where your empathy was both a blessing and a challenge. Perhaps you have found yourself in dynamics where you gave too much, absorbing the emotions and needs of your partner at the expense of your well-being. Or maybe you have encountered relationships that left you feeling drained and unappreciated. These experiences, while challenging, are fertile ground for learning and growth. To glean insights from past relationships, start the process with compassion and curiosity, avoiding judgment or regret. Pose questions such as, "What did these relationships teach me about my emotional needs and boundaries?" Recognizing patterns is crucial. Did prioritizing a partner's needs over personal well-being become a recurring theme? Was there a consistent lack of emotional reciprocity?

Understanding these patterns is pivotal for empaths. It aids in identifying values within relationships, ensuring that personal needs are honored and not compromised. Additionally, recognizing communication dynamics is essential. Reflect on how effectively needs and feelings were conveyed. Did fear of conflict or misunderstanding hinder open and honest expression? For empaths, finding a voice that is both compassionate and assertive is paramount.

Also, think about the lessons learned from the end of relationships. Endings, despite their challenges, often offer profound teachings. What did these endings teach you about resilience, self-worth, and the importance of emotional compatibility? Sometimes, the most challenging endings can lead to the most significant personal growth.

Let us consider a real-life scenario that many empaths can relate to. Imagine Mary, an empath who found herself in a relationship with Isaac, a charming and charismatic individual. Initially, Mary was drawn to Isaac's vibrant personality, feeling an intense emotional connection. However, as time passed, she began to notice a pattern. Mary found herself constantly adjusting her needs and emotions to accommodate Isaac. She would often feel drained after their interactions, yet she could not pinpoint why. Isaac was not overtly unkind, but there was an undercurrent of emotional imbalance in their relationship. Mary often felt unheard and undervalued, yet she continued to invest her emotional energy, hoping things would change. It was not until the relationship ended that Mary took the time to reflect. She realized that she had been so attuned to Isaac's needs and emotions that she had neglected her own. This pattern was not new; it was something she had experienced in past relationships but had not fully acknowledged.

Through this reflection, Mary learned several key lessons. She recognized the importance of maintaining her emotional boundaries and the need to be with someone who not only appreciated her empathy but also reciprocated it. She understood that her tendency to prioritize her partner's needs was rooted in a fear of conflict and a deep-seated desire to be needed. This realization was a turning point for Mary. She began to approach relationships with a new perspective, valuing her own needs and emotions as much as she valued those of others. She learned to communicate more assertively, expressing her feelings and boundaries clearly. This shift not only improved her romantic relationships but also had a positive impact on her friendships and family dynamics.

Mary's story is a powerful example of how reflecting on past relationships can provide valuable insights for empaths. It highlights the importance of understanding one's emotional patterns, setting healthy boundaries, and seeking emotional reciprocity in relationships.

Achieving Inner Peace and Clarity

In the journey of an empath, the encounter with a narcissist can be likened to navigating a stormy sea. The waves of manipulation and emotional turmoil threaten to capsize the boat of inner peace and clarity. As someone who has walked this path, I want to share with you the profound importance of finding calm in this chaos and the personal insights that have guided me through these turbulent waters.

Dealing with a narcissist, especially for an empath, is a complex and often painful experience. The narcissist's need for admiration and lack of empathy can create a toxic dynamic, where the empath feels perpetually drained, undervalued, and misunderstood. I remember feeling like a shadow of myself, constantly trying to appease and accommodate, losing sight of my own needs and feelings in the process.

The first step toward achieving inner peace in such a scenario is recognizing the nature of the relationship. It took me a long time to understand that the emotional imbalance was not my fault, nor was it something I could fix. Narcissists often create a cycle of dependency and control, making it difficult for empaths to maintain their sense of self. Acknowledging this was both painful and liberating. Once I recognized the dynamics at play, the journey to inner peace involved a conscious effort to detach and protect my emotional well-being. This meant setting firm boundaries, a task that was incredibly challenging given my empathic nature. I had to learn to say "no," to prioritize my mental health, and to step back from the emotional roller coaster that had become my norm.

Finding clarity amid this was like trying to find a lighthouse in a fog. It involved a deep dive into self-reflection, understanding my vulnerabilities, and recognizing the patterns that made me susceptible to such relationships. I had to confront some uncomfortable truths about my self-esteem and my deep-rooted fear of rejection. Achieving inner peace also meant seeking support. Talking to friends, therapists, and support groups helped me realize I was not alone in this experience. These conversations were not just comforting; they were eye-opening, providing me with different perspectives and coping strategies.

Here are some introspective questions designed to guide empaths toward a state of inner tranquility and understanding:

- How can I gently detach myself from the emotional turmoil caused by the narcissist, and what steps can I take to maintain this detachment?

- In moments of stress and confusion, what are my go-to strategies for grounding myself and returning to a state of calm?

- What are the signs that indicate I am losing my sense of inner peace, and how can I recognize and address these signs early?

- How can I cultivate a daily practice of mindfulness or meditation that helps me center my thoughts and emotions, keeping me anchored in my reality?

- What are the self-care activities that most effectively help me to recharge and maintain a sense of inner balance?

- How can I create a supportive environment or network that reinforces my journey toward inner peace, especially when facing challenges in narcissistic relationships?

- What affirmations or positive self-talk can I use to remind myself of my worth and strength, especially in moments of doubt or criticism?

- How can I practice forgiveness, both toward myself and the narcissist, as a way of releasing emotional baggage and moving toward peace?

- In what ways can I reinforce my boundaries to protect my peace of mind and emotional well-being?

- How can I remind myself of my own needs and priorities, ensuring that they are not overshadowed by the demands or manipulations of the narcissist?

Engaging with these questions requires patience and honesty. It is a process of peeling back layers to reveal your core strengths and vulnerabilities. By regularly reflecting on these aspects, you can gradually build a resilient and peaceful inner world, one that stands strong even in the face of challenging relationships.

Making Empowered Decisions

In the labyrinth of life, decision-making can feel elusive, especially after emerging from a relationship with a narcissist. I vividly recall a period of profound confusion, but within it, I discovered invaluable insights and strategies. Here, I share how to reclaim decision-making power, forging choices that resonate with your authentic self.

Recognizing Narcissistic Influence: The initial step toward empowered decision-making is acknowledging the narcissist's influence. Narcissists overshadow thoughts and desires, making it challenging for empaths to discern their own voice. Ask, "Is this decision for me or to appease the narcissist?" This question is pivotal in unraveling your desires from theirs.

Reconnecting With Your Inner Voice: As an empath, your inner voice is potent but may be muted by narcissistic dynamics. Reconnect by creating moments of solitude and reflection. Away from narcissistic influence, explore your true wants, feelings, and beliefs. In these quiet moments, your genuine desires and needs can surface.

The Role of Intuition: Intuition is a compass in the fog of decision-making. Tune into your heightened empathic intuition. If a decision feels inherently wrong, trust that feeling. Restoring trust in your intuition is crucial for empowered decisions.

Seeking External Perspectives: Gaining outside perspectives can be invaluable, enriching your understanding without surrendering decision-making power. Consult trusted friends, family, or a therapist. Their insights provide diverse angles, reinforcing your decision-making process.

Practicing Assertiveness: Empowered decisions often involve saying no to what does not align with well-being or values. Assertiveness, challenging for empaths, can be rebuilt gradually. Practice saying "no" in low-stakes situations to strengthen assertiveness.

Visualizing the Outcome: Visualize decision outcomes, envisaging paths your choices could lead. How does each path feel—peaceful, exciting, or dreadful? Visualization clarifies decisions aligning with your authentic self.

Embracing the Journey: Understand that decision-making is a journey, not a destination. Each choice unfolds self-discovery and empowerment. Some decisions are clear, others complex, but each is an opportunity to learn and grow stronger in making authentic choices.

In conclusion, empowered decision-making for empaths—post-narcissistic relationships—involves reconnecting with your inner voice, trusting intuition, seeking external perspectives, practicing assertiveness, visualizing outcomes, and embracing the journey. It is a path to reclaiming power and living authentically.

Chapter 11:
Overcoming Toxic Relationships

Identifying Toxic Patterns in Relationships

O nce, I met someone who seemed like the embodiment of a perfect partner—charming, attentive, and seemingly empathic. But as time passed, the facade began to crumble, revealing a pattern of manipulation, criticism, and emotional volatility. This experience, painful as it was, taught me the importance of recognizing toxic patterns in relationships, especially those involving narcissists.

Toxic relationships often start like any other, sometimes even seeming more enchanting and intense. However, beneath the surface, there are patterns that, once recognized, can be glaringly obvious. The first sign is often a sense of imbalance—where your feelings, needs, and opinions seem to hold less weight than your partner's. In a relationship with a narcissist, this imbalance becomes more pronounced. Your achievements might be downplayed, your feelings dismissed, and your opinions belittled.

Another hallmark of a toxic relationship is the erosion of your self-esteem. Narcissists are adept at making their partners feel inadequate, often through subtle criticisms or overtly demeaning remarks. You might find yourself constantly questioning your worth and abilities, a far cry from the confident person you once were. Control is a significant factor in these relationships. It can manifest in various ways—from dictating how you should dress or spend your time, to more insidious forms like isolating you from friends and family. This control is often justified under the guise of love or concern, making it harder to recognize and challenge.

The cycle of idealization and devaluation is particularly damaging. One moment, you are the center of their world, showered with affection and praise. The next, you are facing cold indifference or cruel criticism. This unpredictable cycle can create a confusing, almost addictive dynamic, where you find yourself constantly striving for the "highs" and dreading the "lows." Gaslighting, a form of psychological manipulation where the abuser makes you question your reality, is another toxic pattern. It can be as blatant as denying an event that occurred or as subtle as twisting words and situations to make you doubt your perceptions and sanity. Emotional volatility is also common. Outbursts of anger, mood swings, or emotional withdrawal can all be mechanisms to keep you off-balance and more easily controlled. In such an environment, walking on eggshells becomes the norm, as you try to avoid any behavior that might trigger a negative response.

To deepen your understanding and help you identify whether you are in a toxic relationship, consider reflecting on these questions:

- Do you feel that your needs and feelings are often sidelined for your partner's? Are your opinions and desires given equal importance, or do they seem to always take a backseat?

- How has your relationship affected your self-esteem? Do you feel more confident and valued, or do you often feel inadequate or unworthy?

- Are there aspects of your life where you feel controlled or restricted by your partner? Does this control extend to your personal choices, friendships, and time?

- Do you experience extreme highs and lows in your relationship? How do these cycles affect your emotional well-being?

- Are there instances where you have felt confused about your memory or perception because of your partner's remarks? Do you often find yourself questioning your sanity or reality in the relationship?

- How stable are the emotional expressions in your relationship? Do you find yourself constantly trying to avoid certain topics or actions for fear of triggering a negative response?

- How does communication unfold in your relationship? Is there open and honest dialogue, or do you often feel unheard and misunderstood?

- Has this relationship positively contributed to your personal growth, or do you feel stifled and diminished?

- How does this relationship align with your future aspirations and the life you wish to lead? Does it support your dreams and goals, or does it hinder them?

- Lastly, do you feel a sense of joy and peace in this relationship, or is it overshadowed by anxiety, fear, and uncertainty?

Reflecting on these questions can provide valuable insights into the dynamics of your relationship. It is a process of self-discovery, helping you to recognize patterns that may be harmful and guiding you toward healthier, more fulfilling relationships.

The Role of Self-Love in Healing

In the journey of healing from a toxic relationship, particularly one involving a narcissist, fostering self-love is akin to tending to a garden after a harsh winter. The essential nourishment for this rejuvenation lies in the practice of turning inward and consistently affirming one's worth and dignity.

In the context of healing, self-love commences with a profound and compassionate acceptance of oneself. It involves facing the mirror, acknowledging the pain, the scars, and the strength that has emerged from the experience. For me, this meant a daily ritual of standing before the mirror, looking into my own eyes, and declaring, "I am enough. I am worthy of love and respect just as I am." This practice of self-affirmation is a potent tool in the healing process, a means of rewriting the narrative that a toxic relationship may have imposed. Where messages of inadequacy or unworthiness once prevailed, you now sow seeds of affirmation and self-compassion. These affirmations act as gentle reminders of your value, contributing to the rebuilding of self-esteem that may have been eroded.

Another dimension of self-love in healing involves cultivating enjoyment in your own company. Post-toxic relationship, there often exists a void that the other person once filled. Filling this void with self-love means discovering joy in solitude—engaging in activities you genuinely enjoy, not merely for distraction but to reconnect with yourself. Whether it is reading, taking leisurely walks, painting, or simply sitting in silence, these moments of solitude become expressions of self-love.

Additionally, self-love encompasses honoring your emotional needs. Permitting yourself to feel a range of emotions without judgment is vital. It involves allowing yourself to grieve, be angry, experience sadness, and also find moments of happiness and hope. Recognizing and validating your emotions is an act of self-respect, an acknowledgment of your shared human experience. Furthermore, self-love in the healing process involves celebrating your progress, no matter how small. Each step forward, every moment of understanding, and every act of kindness toward yourself deserves recognition. It is about acknowledging the strength required for healing and taking pride in the resilience you are cultivating.

Here are some affirmations that you can incorporate into your routine, designed to foster a deep and enduring sense of self-love:

- I am worthy of love and respect, just as I am.

- My feelings and emotions are valid and important.

- I embrace my strengths and accept my weaknesses with compassion.

- I am a beautiful person, both inside and out.

- I deserve happiness and joy in my life.

- I am capable of achieving my dreams and goals.

- Every day, I grow stronger and more resilient.

- I am deserving of time and space for self-care.

- My worth is not defined by others' opinions or expectations.

- I am a unique individual with much to offer the world.

- I choose to focus on love and positivity in my life.

- I am deserving of healthy and fulfilling relationships.

- I trust in my ability to navigate life's challenges.

- I allow myself to follow my own path.

- I am more than enough just as I am.

- I welcome peace and tranquility into my heart and mind.

- My empathic nature is a gift and a strength.

- I am confident in my decisions and trust my intuition.

- I am deserving of success and prosperity.

- I release self-doubt and embrace self-assurance.

- My voice is valuable and my contributions matter.

- I am surrounded by an abundance of love.

- I have the power to create positive change in my life.

- I am deserving of rest.

- I celebrate my unique qualities and talents.

- I am a source of strength and inspiration for myself and others.

- I radiate confidence, positivity, and love.

- I am connected to an endless source of inner peace.

- I accept and love myself unconditionally.

- Every day is a new opportunity to grow and thrive.

Avoiding Future Toxic Entanglements

Navigating the complex terrain of relationships is a particularly vital task for empaths, whose deep sensitivity to the emotions of others can often lead them into entanglements that are emotionally taxing or even toxic. The profound impact of these relationships on an empath's well-being makes it essential to understand and actively avoid such toxic dynamics. It is not just about self-protection; it is about ensuring that your emotional environment is nurturing, supportive, and conducive to your growth.

Toxic relationships, especially those with narcissistic individuals, can be like emotional quicksand for an empath. They often start with a deceptive allure, drawing you in with the promise of deep connection and understanding. However, they can quickly turn into a cycle of emotional manipulation and exploitation, leaving you drained and confused. In such relationships, the empath's compassionate nature is often taken advantage of, leading to a one-sided emotional labor that is neither acknowledged nor reciprocated.

The importance of steering clear of these toxic relationships cannot be overstated. Each negative interaction in such a relationship can chip away at your self-esteem, cloud your judgment, and even alter your perception of healthy interpersonal dynamics. Over time, this can lead to a diminished sense of self-worth and a skewed perspective on what you deserve in a relationship. Therefore, equipping yourself with the knowledge of what constitutes a healthy relationship is crucial. Recognizing and adhering to healthy relationship patterns not only protects you from potential harm but also paves the way for fulfilling and enriching connections. These patterns serve as beacons, guiding you toward interactions that respect and celebrate your empathic nature, rather than exploit it.

In the following list of 20 patterns, you will find the hallmarks of healthy relationships. These patterns are designed to help you identify and nurture connections that are mutually respectful, supportive, and empowering. By internalizing these patterns, you can start to build a future where your relationships are sources of strength, joy, and growth.

1. Mutual respect and admiration, where both individuals value each other's qualities.

2. Honest and open communication, allowing for the expression of needs and concerns without fear.

3. Reciprocal emotional support, ensuring that each person feels nurtured and understood.

4. Independence and personal space, recognizing the importance of maintaining individual identities.

5. Deep-seated trust, rooted in consistent actions and integrity.

6. Constructive conflict resolution, focusing on understanding and collaboration.

7. Encouragement of personal growth, where each person inspires the other to evolve and develop.

8. Balanced giving and receiving, ensuring neither person consistently overextends themselves.

9. Alignment of core values and life goals, fostering a sense of partnership and shared direction.

10. Experiences of joy and comfort, with the relationship serving as a source of happiness and refuge.

11. Empathy and emotional intelligence, allowing for a deeper understanding of each other's experiences.

12. Respect for boundaries, acknowledging and honoring each other's limits and needs.

13. Shared laughter and fun, enjoying light-hearted moments together.

14. Support for each other's passions and interests, celebrating each other's successes and endeavors.

15. Kindness and compassion, treating each other with warmth and understanding.

16. Willingness to apologize and forgive, recognizing and rectifying mistakes.

17. Genuine interest in each other's well-being, showing concern for each other's physical and mental health.

18. Consistency in actions and behavior, creating a sense of reliability and predictability.

19. Presence and attentiveness, being fully engaged during the time spent together.

20. Mutual effort in maintaining the relationship, with both individuals invested in its growth and longevity.

Healing From Past Relationship Traumas

The journey of healing from past relationship traumas is akin to navigating through a dense forest, finding new paths, and discovering hidden strengths along the way. Each step is a move toward a place of inner peace and renewed self-confidence. To commence this healing odyssey, consider harnessing the power of narrative therapy. This entails revisiting the story of your past relationship and rewriting it from a stance of strength and empowerment. Instead of viewing yourself as a victim, adopt the identity of a survivor. Reframe the experience by reflecting on the lessons learned and the personal growth achieved. This narrative transformation can reshape your perception of the past, guiding you to see it not as a series of defeats but as a challenging expedition that has fortified your resilience and wisdom.

Partake in creative expression as a means of healing. Whether through writing, painting, music, or any art form that resonates with you, the act of creation can be profoundly therapeutic. It provides a constructive and deeply satisfying outlet to express and process complex emotions, facilitating the externalization of feelings and thoughts that may be challenging to articulate in words.

Consider exploring mindfulness and meditation, not just as tools for relaxation, but as practices for fostering a deeper connection with your inner self. Mindfulness can help you stay grounded in the present moment, reducing the tendency to ruminate over past hurts. Meditation can offer a space for quiet reflection and inner healing, a sanctuary where you can confront and soothe the emotional turmoil left by past traumas.Look into the concept of self-compassion. This means treating yourself with the same kindness and understanding that you would offer a good friend. Recognize that healing takes time and that it is okay to have moments of weakness or doubt. Practice speaking to yourself with compassion and understanding. Celebrate small victories in your healing journey, and be gentle with yourself on the tougher days. Seek new experiences that broaden your horizons and foster a sense of adventure and joy. This could be anything from traveling to a new place, taking up a new hobby, or even pursuing educational or career opportunities. New experiences can not only provide a welcome distraction but also help in rebuilding your sense of self and your outlook on life.

Finally, consider developing a gratitude practice. This can be as simple as keeping a gratitude journal where you note down things you are thankful for each day. Gratitude can shift your focus from what you have lost to what you still have and can pave the way for a more positive and hopeful outlook on life.

Building a Future With Healthy Relationships

Remember the time when you started a new chapter in a beloved book, filled with anticipation, wondering where the story would take you next? That is a lot like embarking on the journey of building new relationships after overcoming toxic ones. It is a path lined with hope, possibilities, and a bit of uncertainty. After all, once you have navigated the stormy waters of a toxic relationship, the idea of opening your heart again can seem daunting, yet it is also a chance to write a new, healthier narrative for your life.

Imagine you are at the threshold of this new chapter. You have learned, grown, and emerged stronger from your past experiences. Now, you are facing the future with a renewed sense of self and a clear understanding of what you need and deserve in a relationship. This is not just about starting anew; it is about transforming your understanding of relationships based on wisdom gained from past experiences. Let us talk about what this new chapter might look like. Picture relationships where communication flows freely and honestly, where you feel heard and understood, not just for your empathy and compassion but for all that you are. Envision connections where your feelings are respected, where the give-and-take is balanced, and where you can be your true self without fear of judgment or criticism.

One of the most significant steps in this process is learning to trust again. Trust in others and, more importantly, trust in yourself—in your judgment, in your ability to set boundaries, and in your instincts about people. It is about stepping into new relationships with an open heart but also with the wisdom to recognize red flags and the courage to address them.

As you move forward, remember to embrace self-reflection. Reflect on how each new interaction makes you feel, what it teaches you about yourself, and how it aligns with your values and goals for the future. This introspection is a powerful tool for ensuring that your future relationships are healthy, supportive, and fulfilling. Another vital aspect is to surround yourself with a diverse and supportive network. Cultivate friendships and connections that uplift you, provide different perspectives, and encourage your growth. These relationships form a tapestry of support, enriching your life and providing strength and comfort on your journey.

Finally, hold onto hope. Believe in the possibility of love and connection that enriches and elevates. Your past experiences, while challenging, have not diminished your capacity to love and be loved in return. They have instead prepared you for a future where relationships bring joy, growth, and fulfillment. As you embark on this journey of building a future with healthy relationships, carry with you the lessons of the past, the wisdom of the present, and the hope for the future. This new chapter in your life story is yours to write, filled with the promise of healthier, happier relationships.

Chapter 12:
The Path to Self-Love and Acceptance

Understanding the Essence of Self-Love

I n the quiet moments of self-reflection, have you ever considered what self-love truly means to you? For many, especially empaths, the journey to understanding and embracing self-love is often obscured by layers of self-doubt and external expectations. Yet, the essence of self-love is a fundamental pillar in the life of an empath, a beacon guiding them to inner peace and fulfillment. Self-love, in its purest form, is about embracing your worthiness of love and happiness. It is recognizing that you, as much as anyone else in the universe, deserve compassion, understanding, and respect. This realization might seem simple, yet for empaths who often prioritize the emotions and needs of others above their own, it can be a profound revelation.

For an empath, the path to self-love often begins with acknowledging their deep emotional capacity as a strength, not a vulnerability. It is about shifting the perspective from viewing their empathy as a drain on their resources to seeing it as a source of intuitive power and connection. This shift is not just cognitive; it is deeply emotional and transformative. However, understanding self-love is only the first step. Truly embracing it involves a journey of introspection and action. It is about setting boundaries that protect and nurture your emotional well-being. It is learning to say "no" when you are accustomed to always saying "yes," and understanding that self-care is not selfish, but essential.

Additionally, self-love for empaths is about tuning into their own emotions with the same sensitivity and understanding that they offer to others. It is permitting themselves to feel, to be vulnerable, and to seek support when needed. This process can be challenging, as it often involves unlearning patterns of self-neglect and recognizing that their own needs are valid and important.

An essential aspect of self-love is also finding joy in solitude. Empaths are often so attuned to the emotions of others that they can lose themselves in the process. Finding joy in solitude means engaging in activities that replenish their energy and bring them peace, be it through nature, art, meditation, or simply sitting with their thoughts. This is not about isolation but about creating a space where they can reconnect with themselves.

In embracing self-love, empaths unlock a new level of self-awareness and self-acceptance. They start to view themselves with the same compassion and kindness that they offer to the world. This journey might not be easy, but it is undoubtedly rewarding, leading to a life filled with deeper understanding, fulfillment, and a genuine love for oneself.

Practices for Cultivating Self-Love

In the journey of self-love, especially for empaths, it is vital to engage in practices that align with their profound sense of empathy and compassion. Moving away from commonly discussed methods like mindfulness and journaling, let us delve into alternative, yet equally powerful, practices for cultivating self-love.

The first practice involves engaging in empathic self-listening. Dedicate time to sit with your emotions and thoughts, acknowledging them without judgment or an immediate urge to fix or analyze them. Extend to yourself the same level of understanding and empathy naturally granted to others. This may entail quiet moments after a long day, tuning into your emotions, or indulging in a gentle, internal dialogue about your daily experiences.

Another practice entails creating art for self-expression. This transcends traditional art forms, encouraging the use of any creative medium as a tool for conveying your inner world. Whether through crafting, gardening, cooking, or any tactile endeavor, these activities serve as a conduit for expressing complex emotions and thoughts, aiding in their processing and comprehension.

Engaging in self-celebration rituals represents another transformative practice. Actively celebrate your achievements, regardless of size. Treat yourself to something special after reaching a personal goal or take time to acknowledge and relish your successes. This practice serves to reinforce your belief in your capabilities and inherent worth.

Practicing assertive communication is also pivotal. For empaths, accustomed to prioritizing others' needs and opinions, learning to express their thoughts and needs assertively marks a significant stride toward self-love. This does not imply aggression or confrontation; rather, it involves clarity and honesty in articulating feelings and expectations respectfully.

Nature connection exercises offer immense therapeutic benefits. Beyond a simple stroll in the park, this practice involves actively engaging with the environment—touching tree bark, feeling the soil, listening to leaves rustle, and immersing oneself in the natural world. This connection provides a grounding sense and a reminder of one's place in the broader tapestry of life.

Lastly, practicing gratitude toward oneself is essential. While expressions of gratitude are often directed outward, acknowledging one's resilience, kindness, efforts, and growth is equally crucial. This practice revolves around recognizing and appreciating one's own value and contribution to the world.

Each of these practices presents a distinct pathway to foster self-love. They offer empaths opportunities to forge deep and meaningful connections with themselves, reinforcing the belief in their inherent worth and strength.

Conquering Internalized Negativity

Envision an empath, naturally attuned to others' emotions, entangled in a relationship with a narcissist—a dynamic marked by a significant imbalance. The empath's genuine desire to please and support becomes a consistent source of admiration for the narcissist, who, lacking empathy, offers little emotional sustenance in return. This sets in motion a cycle where self-criticism and negativity embed themselves in the empath's psyche. Negativity in such relationships often operates subtly and insidiously. Skilled at manipulation, narcissists adeptly shift blame onto the empath, who, over time, internalizes this negativity. The empath starts believing they are at fault, not good enough, or that they must strive harder to meet unattainable expectations. This persistent self-criticism becomes a constant backdrop, eroding self-esteem and a sense of worth. Empaths in these relationships may also grapple with constant questioning of their perceptions and feelings, a result of gaslighting. This intensifies self-doubt and negativity, transforming the once vibrant and intuitive empath into a shadow lost in self-criticism and confusion.

What steps can be taken? Recognition is paramount—the understanding that the negativity and self-criticism are not reflections of true worth but outcomes of a deeply imbalanced relationship. The next step involves reclaiming one's narrative and disentangling self-worth from the narcissist's approval or disapproval. It is a process of relearning to trust feelings and judgments, honoring intuition, and validating emotions. This often necessitates support from trusted friends, therapists, or support groups.

Ultimately, it is about rewriting the script of self-criticism into one of self-compassion. Replace negative self-talk with affirmations of strengths, capabilities, and worth. Acknowledge that empathy is a gift, not a liability—a trait fostering deep connections and understanding. When directed inward, empathy becomes a potent source of healing and self-acceptance. Escaping the grip of negativity and self-criticism in relationships with narcissists is a journey toward healing and profound self-appreciation. It leads to a space where the empath can fully and joyfully embrace their empathic nature. This journey is undoubtedly worthwhile.

Embracing and Celebrating Your Uniqueness

There is a unique beauty in being different, in having a trait that sets you apart from the crowd. For those who are empaths, this uniqueness is found in their profound ability to feel and understand the emotions of others. It is a trait that, while sometimes challenging, is a remarkable gift—one that allows for connections and understandings that are deep and rich.

Think of it this way: In a world where so many strive to fit in, your empathic nature makes you stand out. It is like having a secret lens that lets you see into people's hearts and minds, understanding their joys, sorrows, and fears on a level that others might not perceive. This ability is not just unique; it is a superpower in its own right. But embracing this part of yourself means more than just acknowledging it; it is about celebrating it. Take a moment to reflect on the times when your empathy has allowed you to connect with someone else's pain or happiness, to be there for them in a way that was genuinely needed. These are the moments that showcase the beauty of your gift.

Your uniqueness also lies in the way you experience the world. You might find beauty in the smallest things, feel the pain of a stranger as if it were your own, or have an innate understanding of the complexities of human emotions. These experiences, though sometimes overwhelming, are what makes your perspective on life rich and invaluable.

It is also important to remember that your empathic nature is just one aspect of who you are. You have a whole universe of qualities, talents, and dreams that make you the person you are. Embracing your uniqueness means exploring these other aspects of yourself, cultivating your interests, and nurturing your talents.

In a world that often feels disconnected, your ability to empathize is a bridge that connects you deeply with others. It is a quality that should be celebrated and cherished. So, wear your empathy like a badge of honor. Be proud of your ability to feel deeply, to understand others, and to bring a little more empathy into the world. In celebrating your uniqueness, you not only affirm your value but also inspire others to recognize and cherish their own unique traits. It sets off a ripple effect of acceptance and self-love that can make the world a touch kinder, a tad more understanding, and a bit more empathic.

Creating a Self-Care Routine

As you continue to embrace and celebrate your unique empathic qualities, establishing a self-care routine becomes an integral part of nurturing both your physical and emotional well-being. Self-care is not just an act of maintaining health; it is a testament to the respect and love you hold for yourself. Think of self-care as crafting a personal sanctuary, a space where you can retreat, recharge, and reconnect with yourself. This sanctuary is not necessarily a physical space; it can be a routine or a set of practices that you integrate into your daily life. The key is to make these practices regular and meaningful, tailored to your specific needs and preferences.

Start by considering activities that help you unwind and decompress. For some, this might be a quiet walk in nature, allowing the stillness and beauty of the outdoors to provide a soothing backdrop for reflection. For others, it could be a warm bath, a yoga session, or simply sitting quietly with a cup of tea. The aim is to find activities that bring you a sense of peace and relaxation.

Nutrition and physical health are also crucial components of self-care. Paying attention to what you eat, ensuring a balanced and nourishing diet, and engaging in regular physical activity are all ways of showing love and care for your body. Remember, your physical well-being is deeply connected to your emotional health. Sleep is another vital aspect of self-care. Ensure that you are getting enough restful sleep, as it plays a critical role in both your physical and mental health. Create a bedtime routine that signals to your body that it is time to wind down and rest, whether that is through reading, meditation, or gentle stretching.

Do not forget the importance of social self-care. This involves spending time with people who uplift and support you, who understand and appreciate your empathic nature. These interactions should leave you feeling rejuvenated and valued, not drained or undervalued.

Lastly, remember that self-care is an ongoing process. It is about continually checking in with yourself, assessing your needs, and being willing to adjust your routine as those needs change. It is about committing yourself to treat yourself with the same compassion and care that you offer so readily to others. In establishing a self-care routine, you are not just maintaining your well-being; you are affirming your worth and embracing the importance of keeping your cup full. It is a crucial step in ensuring that you can continue to share your empathic gifts with the world without sacrificing your health and happiness.

Chapter 13:
Healing and Personal Growth

The Stages of the Healing Journey

T he path to healing, especially for empaths who have traversed the complexities of toxic relationships, is far from a linear trajectory. It unfolds with a tapestry of emotions and experiences, revealing both challenges and insights. Understanding the healing process is paramount, acknowledging its non-linear nature—marked by ebbs and flows, encompassing both progress and setbacks.

The initial step in this healing odyssey involves recognizing and embracing the pain and the repercussions of the toxic relationship. It entails permitting oneself to fully experience the hurt, anger, and confusion that accompany the conclusion of such a detrimental connection. This acknowledgment is pivotal, validating the individual's experience and laying the groundwork for profound healing.

Following this is the phase of understanding and acceptance. It necessitates a critical examination of the past relationship, identifying toxic patterns, and understanding their impact. While a challenging step, it is indispensable for learning from the past and preventing the recurrence of similar patterns in the future. Acceptance, in this context, does not signify approval but rather an acknowledgment of what transpired and its influence on personal growth.

Subsequently, the healing process involves detachment and the release of the emotional grip the relationship may still hold. This proves to be the most demanding part, requiring the relinquishment not only of the person but also of the myriad "what-ifs" and "should-haves" that often linger after a toxic relationship. It is a matter of reconciling with the necessity of moving forward for one's well-being.

An integral facet of this healing stage is the rediscovery of one's identity outside the confines of the relationship. Toxic connections often leave empaths questioning their self-worth and identity. Reconnecting with personal interests, passions, and strengths is imperative. This phase centers on rebuilding a sense of self and reclaiming independence.

The final step is transformation—the essence of true healing. It involves utilizing the lessons learned to grow and evolve. This transformation goes beyond merely avoiding similar situations in the future; it encompasses building stronger, healthier relationships. It stands as a testament to one's resilience and strength.

Throughout this intricate process, practicing self-compassion and exercising patience are critical. Healing is a time-consuming journey accompanied by moments of doubt and frustration. It is crucial to remember that each step, irrespective of its size, signifies progress on the path toward healing and growth.

Emotional Release and Letting Go

At times, in the quiet aftermath of a storm, we find ourselves amid the remnants of what was once a significant part of our lives. For empaths emerging from the tumult of a toxic relationship, this aftermath is not just about picking up the pieces; it is about allowing ourselves to feel the full range of emotions left in the wake of that storm—and then letting them go.

The concept of emotional release is both straightforward and intricate. It involves allowing oneself to fully experience emotions and acknowledging them without judgment or fear. While simple in its call for self-honesty, it is complex due to the need to untangle the web of feelings accumulated over time. This cathartic process demands both courage and honesty.

In toxic relationships, emotions are often suppressed, manipulated, or neglected. As an empath, you may have set aside your feelings to accommodate the needs of your partner. Now, in the aftermath of that relationship, those suppressed emotions resurface with unexpected intensity. Emotional release is an opportunity to confront these feelings head-on. It is important to understand that emotional release is not a sign of weakness; it is quite the opposite. It is an act of strength. It is about taking control of your emotional well-being and refusing to let past hurts dictate your current state of mind. This process is about honoring your feelings, giving them the space to be expressed, and then gently letting them go.

Letting go does not imply forgetting or dismissing what happened; rather, it signifies acceptance. While those experiences were part of your journey, they need not define your future. Letting go is understanding that you possess the power to move beyond the pain, learn from it, and emerge stronger.

Below is an exercise that will help in the emotional release process, providing a structured approach for empaths to let go of negative emotions and find inner peace.

Meditation for Emotional Relief:

1. Choose a comfortable and quiet place for your meditation, somewhere you feel safe and undisturbed.

2. Sit or lie down in a comfortable position. Gently close your eyes and start to focus on your breathing. Take deep, slow breaths, and with each exhale, consciously relax your body.

3. Visualize roots growing from the base of your spine or feet, extending deep into the earth. Feel the grounding energy of the earth providing you with stability and strength.

4. Bring to mind the emotions you are seeking to release. Allow yourself to feel and acknowledge each emotion without judgment or criticism.

5. Imagine each emotion as a colored stream of light within you. With each inhale, see these colors becoming more vivid, and with each exhale, envision them flowing out of your body, dispersing into the air and fading away.

6. Silently or aloud, affirm your intention to release these emotions. You might say something like, "I acknowledge these

emotions and I let them go. They do not control me. I release them to find peace."

7. Picture a soothing, gentle light, perhaps white or soft blue, entering your body with each inhale. Feel this calming light filling the spaces left by the released emotions, bringing with it tranquility and renewal.

8. Express gratitude to yourself for taking this time to face and release these emotions, recognizing your courage and strength.

9. Slowly bring your awareness back to the present moment. Start by becoming aware of the physical sensations in your body, and then gently move your fingers and toes.

10. When you feel ready, open your eyes, bringing with you a sense of calmness and emotional lightness from the meditation.

11. After the meditation, consider spending a few minutes in quiet reflection or journaling, noting any insights or feelings that emerged during the practice.

Rebuilding Confidence and Self-Esteem

Embarking on the path of recovery after a relationship with a narcissist, empaths stand at a critical juncture that demands more than mere healing—it necessitates a profound transformation. This transformative journey is not just a return to self; it is an odyssey interweaving the rediscovery of personal identity, the celebration of individual achievements, the cultivation of self-respect, and the triumphant conquering of the fear of judgment. For empaths who have weathered the storm of emotional manipulation and imbalance, this marks a pivotal moment in reclaiming their power and voice.

This challenging yet growth-rich journey provides opportunities for self-realization and turning the pain of the past into present strength. In this process, empaths redefine their sense of self-worth, no longer through the lens of the narcissist but through their own renewed and resilient perspective.

The cornerstone of this transformation is rediscovering personal identity, peeling back the layers of the relationship to reveal the essence of oneself, separate from the influence of the past partner. This exploration entails patience and curiosity, where each step, whether revisiting an old hobby or embracing a new interest, brings one closer to understanding the authentic self. As the reconnection with personal identity unfolds, recognition and celebration of personal achievements become integral. Each accomplishment, whether significant or modest, represents a milestone in the journey of self-reclamation. Celebrating these achievements is crucial, shifting the focus from endured challenges to accomplished triumphs—a process reinforcing the notion that, despite faced difficulties, one possesses the strength and resilience to overcome and thrive.

Integral to this transformative journey is the cultivation of self-respect—a practice of honoring needs, establishing healthy boundaries, and treating oneself with kindness. This ongoing process involves recognizing intrinsic worth and refusing to accept less than deserved, asserting dignity and value not only to the world but also to oneself.

However, this path is not devoid of challenges. Overcoming the fear of judgment, particularly after enduring a relationship where actions and thoughts were constantly scrutinized, poses a significant hurdle. This fear can be paralyzing, but overcoming it is empowering. It involves embracing the fact that one's worth is not contingent on others' opinions, building trust in one's judgment and decisions, and finding comfort in staying true to oneself.

These interconnected steps—rediscovering identity, celebrating achievements, cultivating self-respect, and overcoming the fear of judgment—constitute the foundation for rebuilding confidence and self-esteem. They are the essential building blocks of a newly empowered self—one that recognizes and embraces its worth, strength, and resilience.

Reflecting on the journey after a relationship with a narcissist is akin to sifting through the ashes of a fire. Initially revealing destruction, closer examination yields not only remnants but also hard-earned, precious lessons. These lessons extend beyond understanding what went wrong; they offer insights into how one loves, gives, and, importantly, stands up for oneself. Being with a narcissist can feel like walking on a tightrope, balancing one's needs with their demands. Yet, within this balancing act, lessons emerge. Setting boundaries, saying "no," and valuing personal feelings as much as those of others become vital. Each reflection on the discomfort of the past builds a map guiding compassionate behavior without losing oneself—a potent lesson.

There is also the recognition of one's strength. Emerging from a storm, battered but not broken, demonstrates resilience—an inner strength that was perhaps previously underestimated. It is akin to discovering a hidden well of fortitude. Recognizing red flags and understanding the signs of manipulation is another valuable lesson. It is akin to developing a sixth sense that alerts one to emotional danger, offering protection for navigating relationships more wisely in the future.

Perhaps the most beautiful lesson is the rewriting of one's story. Moving from a narrative of victimhood to one of survival and growth is a realization that the painful past chapter does not dictate the end of one's story. With the pen in hand, one can write the next chapters.

In the end, these lessons are not just about moving past a toxic relationship; they are about evolution and becoming more authentic. It is a journey with its ups and downs, but each step, each lesson, propels one toward a stronger, more self-aware self.

Discovering Happiness and Purpose Following Abuse

After the turmoil of a toxic relationship, finding your way back to joy and purpose can seem like a distant dream. Yet, it is in this very journey of rediscovery that many empaths find a deeper, more authentic sense of happiness and fulfillment.

To begin, let us explore the reconnection with joy. Often, joy resides in the overlooked simplicity of everyday moments. Take notice of these instances—the sun's warmth on your skin, the laughter shared with a friend, the satisfaction derived from a well-cooked meal. These modest pleasures serve as the foundational elements of joy, reminding us that happiness is not an elusive destination but a path walked each day, one step at a time. Rediscovering joy also entails revisiting old passions or exploring new interests. Reflect on activities that once brought you happiness, or delve into novel pursuits that capture your curiosity. Whether it involves art, music, gardening, or hiking, these activities transcend mere hobbies; they act as gateways to joy and self-expression, offering a refuge from the past and a means to engage with the present in a fulfilling manner.

Now, let us delve into the concept of purpose. Following an abusive relationship, your sense of purpose may feel shaken. Understand that your purpose is dynamic, evolving alongside your personal growth. Begin by questioning what holds the most significance for you now. What sparks your passion? What endeavors do you feel compelled to pursue? This might encompass personal objectives, such as improving your health, or broader aspirations, such as volunteering or advocating for a cause close to your heart. Your purpose is uniquely yours, providing a sense of direction and fulfillment. In the pursuit of purpose, recognize the transformative power of assisting others. Empaths possess a natural ability to comprehend and connect with people. Directing this ability toward aiding those in need can be immensely gratifying, serving as a channel for your healing and a source of purpose.

Maintaining a positive outlook is paramount in this journey. Choose to focus on hope and possibilities, steering away from dwelling on past pain. This does not involve dismissing the challenges you have faced; rather, it entails acknowledging them and consciously shifting your focus toward hope and growth. A positive outlook is a conscious choice, empowering you to view life through a lens of potential and opportunity.

Lastly, practice patience with yourself. Rediscovering joy and purpose is a gradual process that unfolds over time. Anticipate days of uncertainty and setbacks, recognizing that these are integral components of the journey and that each incremental step forward, propels you toward a life enriched with joy, purpose, and significance.

The Role of Therapy and Support

Recognizing the pivotal role of therapy and support is paramount as empaths embark on the journey to recovery, especially when healing from the aftermath of a toxic relationship. This intricate and multifaceted process can experience substantial enhancement through the guidance of a professional therapist and the steadfast support of a compassionate network.

Therapy provides a unique and secure space where empaths can unpack their experiences with a skilled professional. It becomes a haven for the safe exploration of the profound emotions and traumas that often linger from a toxic relationship. A therapist well-versed in the dynamics of such relationships can assist empaths in processing their experiences, offering not only empathy but also practical strategies to cope with and heal from these deep emotional wounds. Additionally, therapy introduces a fresh perspective on patterns that may have contributed to the toxic relationship. It involves uncovering and understanding these patterns, equipping empaths with the tools to forge healthier relationships in the future. Therapy becomes instrumental in cultivating new coping mechanisms, fortifying personal boundaries, and reinstating a sense of self-worth that may have been eroded during the relationship.

Beyond the therapist's office, the support of a caring network—comprised of friends, family, and support groups—is equally indispensable. Having individuals who listen, comprehend, and validate your feelings can be profoundly healing. This involves creating a community that uplifts and stands as a testament to the understanding that you are not alone on this journey. Support groups, in particular, offer a sense of solidarity, providing a space where shared experiences lead to mutual understanding and empowerment. This support network also plays a pivotal role in aiding empaths not only in navigating the healing process but in thriving beyond it. It encompasses individuals who encourage the rediscovery of interests, passions, and joys—facets of life that may have taken a backseat during the toxic relationship.

It is crucial to remember that seeking therapy and support is a deeply personal decision that should be made at one's own pace. The focus is on finding the type of help that resonates with you, whether it involves one-on-one counseling, group therapy, or confiding in trusted friends or family members. The objective is to establish a support system that makes you feel heard, understood, and empowered to heal and grow.

Chapter 14:
Cultivating Positive and Healthy New Relationships

Approaching Relationships With Awareness

E mbarking on new relationships after enduring a toxic one unfolds as a journey filled with cautious hope and introspection. For an empath, this fresh chapter signifies not just the pursuit of connection but also an entrance into these relationships with an elevated sense of awareness. This heightened awareness acts as both a shield and a guide, grounded in a profound understanding of past patterns.

Engaging in introspection about past relationships, particularly those that were toxic or harmful, can be uncomfortable yet essential. In these reflective moments, one uncovers patterns—perhaps a tendency to prioritize a partner's needs over one's own or a habit of excusing unacceptable behavior. Recognizing these patterns is the initial step in breaking free from them. It involves identifying the moments when one deviated from their true self and comprehending the reasons behind those choices. This is not a process of self-reproach but rather one of self-discovery.

Approaching new relationships with heightened awareness entails applying these insights. It means being vigilant not only about how others treat you but also about how you respond and react in relationships. Are you falling back into old patterns? Are you compromising your values or boundaries? Awareness becomes the tool that empowers you to navigate these questions, making choices that align with your authentic self. This increased awareness also encompasses a deep understanding of what a healthy relationship looks like for you. It involves recognizing the qualities you value in a partner—honesty, respect, empathy—and actively seeking them rather than just hoping to stumble upon them. This understanding aids in identifying early signs that a relationship may not be healthy, allowing for informed decisions on whether to deepen the connection or step back. Furthermore, this journey of heightened awareness is about cultivating trust in oneself. It entails believing in your ability to make healthier choices in relationships, a trust built over time through experiences and reflections. Each decision, each step taken with conscious awareness, serves to reinforce this trust.

It is crucial to remember that heightened awareness does not mean building impenetrable walls around oneself. It is not about closing off opportunities for love and connection. Instead, it is about moving forward with an open heart and a clear mind, equipped with the wisdom gained from past experiences.

Before stepping into a new relationship, taking a moment to pause and asking key questions can be immensely beneficial. These questions serve as tools for introspection, helping to clarify thoughts, understand needs, and recognize potential patterns from past relationships. The following list of self-reflective questions can guide you in this process:

- What have I learned about myself from my past relationships?

- How do my past experiences influence my current approach to relationships?

- What are the qualities I truly value and seek in a partner?

- Are there any warning signs or red flags that I tend to overlook in relationships?

- How do I typically react when my boundaries are challenged?

- In what ways have I compromised my own needs for the sake of a relationship in the past?

- What does a balanced and healthy relationship look like to me?

- How comfortable am I with expressing my needs and desires to a potential partner?

- What are my non-negotiables in a relationship?

- How do I distinguish between genuine connection and over-attachment?

- In what ways can I maintain my individuality and independence in a relationship?

- How do I plan to protect and nurture my empathic nature in a new relationship?

- What steps will I take if I notice old unhealthy patterns reemerging?

- How will I ensure open and honest communication in my next relationship?

- What does trust mean to me in a relationship, and how do I plan to build it?

By reflecting on these questions, one can gain deeper insights into relationship patterns, needs, and expectations. This introspective process is not just about preparing for a new relationship; it is also about reaffirming one's commitment to self-awareness and personal growth as an empath.

Recognizing and Addressing Warning Signs

Recognizing the significance of early warning signs in new relationships is essential, particularly for individuals who have encountered toxic relationships in the past. These signs often act as precursors, offering insights into potential issues that may escalate into more profound problems down the line. For empaths, characterized by heightened intuition and emotional awareness, early recognition and proactive addressing of these signs play a pivotal role in establishing relationships that are healthy and fulfilling. Here is a list of warning signs:

1. Rapid Intensity: A relationship that intensifies too quickly, often without a solid foundation of trust and understanding.

2. Boundary Disrespect: Your partner consistently ignores or dismisses your boundaries, indicating a lack of respect for your personal space and values.

3. Inconsistent Communication: Fluctuating patterns of communication, such as unexplained absences or non-committal responses, can signal a lack of reliability or commitment.

4. Disrespectful Behavior: Subtle or explicit behaviors that demean or belittle you, eroding your self-esteem and sense of worth.

5. Control Issues: Attempts to control aspects of your life, such as your appearance, social interactions, or decisions, often under the guise of concern.

6. Gaslighting: Making you doubt your perceptions, memories, or feelings, leading to confusion and self-doubt.

7. Lack of Empathy: Failure to show understanding or compassion for your emotions and experiences, indicating emotional disconnect.

8. Excessive Jealousy or Possessiveness: Overbearing jealousy or possessiveness that goes beyond normal concern, leading to restrictive or isolating behaviors.

9. Unresolved Past Issues: Persistent negative patterns from their past relationships, including unresolved conflicts or blaming ex-partners for all past relationship problems.

10. Avoidance of Serious Discussions: Consistently avoiding or deflecting conversations about significant relationship issues or personal challenges.

Once you have identified these warning signs, the next step involves an effective response:

- Trust Your Feelings: If something feels off, trust your instincts. Your emotional intuition is a crucial guide in evaluating relationship dynamics.

- Open Communication: Address concerns with your partner in a respectful, non-confrontational manner. Honest communication can clarify misunderstandings and pave the way for a healthier relationship.

- Enforce Boundaries: Firmly maintain your boundaries. If they are consistently ignored, it is a strong signal of disrespect.

- Seek Outside Perspectives: Discussing your concerns with trusted friends or family can provide additional insights and help you see the situation more objectively.

- Reflect on the Relationship: Consider the implications of these warning signs for your relationship. Are they deal-breakers, or can they be resolved through mutual effort and understanding?

- Professional Guidance: In complex situations, seeking advice from a therapist or counselor can be beneficial in understanding your reactions and planning an effective response.

Being mindful of these early warning signs and responding appropriately is not about paranoia or fear. It is about entering new relationships with a sense of informed caution, ensuring that you are building connections that are respectful, supportive, and enriching.

Key Aspects of Balanced and Healthy Relationships:

Embarking on the journey of a balanced and healthy relationship involves navigating through various fundamental aspects that contribute to the overall well-being of the partnership. These key elements serve as pillars, supporting a connection built on mutual understanding, respect, and shared growth. From open communication and trustworthiness to individual growth and shared values, each aspect plays a crucial role in fostering a relationship that is not only resilient but also enriching. Let us explore these key aspects that form the foundation of balanced and healthy relationships, creating a framework for lasting happiness and fulfillment.

- Mutual Respect: The foundation of any healthy relationship is mutual respect. This means honoring each other's opinions, feelings, and boundaries. It is about acknowledging and valuing the differences that each partner brings to the relationship.

- Effective Communication: Open, honest communication is vital. It involves expressing your needs, desires, and concerns clearly and respectfully. It also means being a good listener, giving your partner the space and attention to voice their thoughts and feelings.

- Maintaining Individuality: A balanced relationship respects the individuality of each partner. It is important to have your own interests, hobbies, and friendships outside of the relationship. This individuality enriches your personal growth and adds depth to the relationship.

- Equal Partnership: A healthy relationship is an equal partnership. Decision-making and responsibilities should be shared. This equality helps prevent one partner from feeling overburdened or underappreciated.

- Support and Encouragement: Encouraging each other's goals and supporting each other through challenges is key. It is about being each other's cheerleader, celebrating successes, and offering comfort and guidance during tough times.

- Trust and Honesty: Trust is the cornerstone of a healthy relationship. Building and maintaining trust involves being honest, reliable, and consistent in your actions and words.

- Healthy Conflict Resolution: Disagreements are natural, but it is how you handle them that matters. Healthy conflict resolution involves addressing issues head-on constructively, without resorting to blame or avoidance.

- Balanced Empathy: For empaths, maintaining a balance in empathy is crucial. While being understanding and compassionate, it is important not to lose yourself in your partner's emotions. Setting emotional boundaries is key to preserving your well-being.

- Nurturing Emotional and Physical Intimacy: A balanced relationship nurtures both emotional and physical intimacy. This includes sharing personal thoughts and feelings, as well as maintaining a fulfilling physical connection.

- Continuous Growth and Learning: A healthy relationship is one that evolves. It involves continuously learning about each other and growing together as a couple. It is about facing life's changes and challenges as a team.

- Respecting Privacy and Space: Every individual needs personal space and time for themselves. Respecting your partner's need for privacy and alone time, as well as asserting your own, is key to a healthy relationship.

- Shared Values and Goals: Having common values and goals can strengthen a relationship. It is about aligning on core beliefs and what you both want for the future, whether it is family, career, or personal growth.

- Flexibility and Adaptability: Life is unpredictable. Being flexible and adaptable in the face of change or unexpected circumstances is important in maintaining a harmonious relationship.

- Showing Appreciation and Gratitude: Regularly expressing appreciation and gratitude for each other can reinforce a positive and loving relationship environment.

- Learning From Mistakes: Every relationship has its ups and downs. Learning from mistakes and being willing to change negative patterns is crucial for a relationship to thrive.

- Reciprocity: A healthy relationship involves a balance of give and take. It is important that both partners feel their contributions, whether emotional, practical, or financial, are acknowledged and reciprocated.

- Emotional Support: Providing emotional support during tough times is crucial. It involves showing empathy, listening without judgment, and offering comfort.

- Celebrating Together: Celebrating achievements, milestones, and happy moments together strengthens the bond and creates shared joyous memories.

- Managing Finances Fairly: How finances are handled can be a significant aspect of a relationship. Discussing and managing financial matters fairly and transparently can prevent many conflicts.

- Compassion and Forgiveness: Being compassionate and willing to forgive minor mistakes or misunderstandings helps in nurturing a loving and lasting relationship.

These elements are not exhaustive but provide a comprehensive guide for empaths and others striving to build relationships that are balanced, healthy, and fulfilling. Each relationship is unique, and what works for one couple may be different for another. The key is open communication, mutual respect, and a willingness to grow together.

Effective Communication and Vulnerability

Have you ever felt like you are walking on a tightrope when it comes to expressing your true feelings in a relationship? You are not alone. Many of us struggle with the balance between being open and protecting ourselves. In this section, we will explore how effective communication and vulnerability are not just beneficial but essential in building trust and intimacy in relationships, especially after experiencing a toxic one.

Imagine you are an artist, and your words are your paintbrush. With each stroke, you have the power to create a masterpiece or a mess. Effective communication in relationships is similar. It is about expressing your thoughts, feelings, and needs in a way that is clear, respectful, and empathic. But how do you do that?

1. Listen Actively: True communication is a two-way street. Listening actively means fully engaging with what your partner is saying, without planning your response or judgment. It is about understanding their perspective, even if you do not agree.

2. Speak Your Truth: Be honest about your feelings and needs. It is okay to say, "I feel hurt when you do this," or "I need some time to myself." Remember, expressing your truth is not about blaming but about sharing your inner world.

3. Non-Verbal Cues Matter: Communication is not just about words. Your body language, tone of voice, and even your silence speak volumes. Be mindful of the non-verbal messages you are sending.

Vulnerability is like opening the window of your soul and letting someone see the real you. It is scary, but it is also where deep connections are formed. Brené Brown, a renowned researcher, describes vulnerability as the birthplace of love, belonging, joy, courage, empathy, and creativity. To embrace vulnerability in your relationships:

1. Start Small: Share something personal, but not too deep. It could be a fear, a dream, or a memory. This builds trust and encourages your partner to open up too.

2. Accept Imperfection: Both you and your partner are human, which means you are both beautifully imperfect. Embrace this fact and be gentle with each other's vulnerabilities.

3. Create a Safe Space: Ensure that your relationship is a safe space for both of you to be vulnerable. This means no judgment, no ridicule, and a lot of understanding and support.

Expressing needs in a new relationship, especially after a toxic one, can be fraught with challenges. You might fear rejection or feel guilty for having needs. Remember, it is healthy and necessary to express your needs in a relationship. If you find it difficult, consider seeking support from a therapist or a support group. They can provide you with tools and strategies to communicate more effectively.

Regaining Trust After Toxic Relationships

The path to regaining trust in the wake of a toxic relationship is both delicate and profound. It involves healing from past wounds and gradually opening up to new possibilities of connection. Despite its challenges, this journey offers a significant opportunity for personal growth and a deeper understanding of oneself.

An essential initial step involves acknowledging and processing the emotions stemming from the toxic relationship. Embracing the range of feelings that naturally arise is crucial for the healing process. Additionally, reflecting on the past relationship is vital, not for assigning blame but for gaining insights and learning from the experience.

At the core of this transformative process is the cultivation of self-trust. Foundational for future relationships, this involves believing in one's judgment and decisions. Self-trust is nurtured through introspection, understanding core values, and identifying genuine desires in a relationship. Part of this journey also entails forgiving oneself, particularly for any lingering guilt about not recognizing the toxicity earlier.

When it comes to establishing new connections, a cautious and mindful approach is key. While the temptation to rush into fresh relationships may be strong, genuine trust is built over time through consistent and honest interactions. Open communication about one's journey and needs can foster mutual understanding and patience with a new partner.

A supportive and healthy environment is vital for trust to flourish. Clearly defined boundaries are essential, not only for protecting emotional well-being but also for establishing respect and understanding in a new relationship. A robust support network, comprising friends, family, or professionals, serves as a pillar of stability and encouragement.

Lastly, embracing vulnerability is a courageous step toward building meaningful connections. Despite the perceived intimidation, especially after past betrayals, vulnerability proves crucial for fostering intimacy and trust in any relationship.

This journey transcends the act of moving past a challenging chapter; it encompasses growth, learning, and the courage to once again embrace love and trust. It is a process that demands patience, self-awareness, and a willingness to take a chance on new beginnings.

Chapter 15:
Personal Development and Empathic Growth

Opportunities for Personal Growth After Narcissistic Relationships

After the end of a narcissistic relationship, it might feel like you are emerging from a long, challenging journey. Yet, this period in your life can unexpectedly become a profound opportunity for personal growth and self-discovery. This section explores how the experiences, as difficult as they were, can lead to significant personal transformation and empowerment.

The Path to Self-Discovery: The space left by a relationship that once consumed so much of your emotional energy can be transformed into a canvas for rediscovery. This is a time to reconnect with your inner self and explore your passions, dreams, and desires that might have been overshadowed. It is about asking yourself key questions about your identity and happiness and gently uncovering the layers to reveal your true self, perhaps a self you are meeting for the first time.

From Pain to Empowerment: The journey through and out of a narcissistic relationship, while painful, offers a unique opportunity to build emotional strength and resilience. This process involves reshaping your narrative from one of victimhood to one of survival and growth. It is about recognizing your journey, acknowledging your strength, and understanding that you have emerged more resilient.

Reconnecting With Your Inner Voice: In a relationship where your voice might have been overshadowed, there is now a valuable opportunity to reconnect with and trust your inner wisdom. This is about tuning into your intuition, learning to trust your judgments, and making decisions that resonate with your true self. It is a powerful reaffirmation of your autonomy and a step toward regaining control over your life.

Joy in Creativity and Expression: Engaging in creative activities offers a way to process and express your emotions, providing a therapeutic outlet and a path to rediscovering joy and passion. Whether it is through art, writing, music, or any other form of creativity, these pursuits allow you to reclaim your voice and find solace and joy in expression.

A New Perspective on Life: Emerging from a challenging relationship often leads to a profound shift in how you view life. This new perspective can bring about a deeper appreciation for simple joys, a more empathic understanding of others, and a renewed sense of gratitude. It is about seeing the world not just as a place of challenges but as one rich with opportunities for growth and happiness.

The end of a narcissistic relationship, while challenging, opens the door to a journey filled with self-discovery, empowerment, and a deeper appreciation for life. It is an opportunity to emerge, not just healed but transformed and renewed.

Developing Emotional Intelligence and Resilience

Navigating the path of personal development, particularly after the end of a challenging relationship, often leads to an enriching journey centered on nurturing emotional intelligence and resilience. These two deeply interconnected skills are essential for anyone seeking to understand themselves better and interact with the world in a more balanced and fulfilling way.

The journey begins with emotional intelligence; the skill of understanding and managing your own emotions and empathizing with others. This process starts from within, through a deep and honest exploration of your emotional landscape. Recognizing and naming your emotions is the first step toward understanding them. This self-awareness is crucial as it allows you to navigate your feelings without being overwhelmed, enabling informed and emotionally clear decision-making. But emotional intelligence is not just about introspection; it also involves looking outward with empathy. Understanding and sharing the feelings of others not only strengthens your relationships but also enriches your emotional understanding. This dual focus—inward on your emotions and outward on those of others—creates a balanced approach to emotional intelligence.

Alongside emotional intelligence is the equally important skill of resilience—the ability to recover and bounce back from adversity. Resilience is built on the foundation of accepting that life is replete with challenges and setbacks. This acceptance is empowering, as it shifts your perspective from feeling victimized by circumstances to actively engaging with them. A key component of resilience is the support network you cultivate. Having people who provide understanding and support is invaluable during tough times, acting as a pillar of strength and stability. Another aspect of resilience is the ability to learn from past experiences. Viewing challenges as opportunities for growth and reflection enriches your life experience and prepares you for future obstacles. This learning is not just about intellectual understanding but also about emotional growth. It is about taking the lessons learned from each challenge and using them to build a stronger, more adaptable version of yourself.

Underpinning both emotional intelligence and resilience is the practice of self-care. Regularly engaging in activities that nurture your physical, emotional, and mental well-being is crucial. This self-care is a form of self-respect; it acknowledges the importance of your well-being and its role in maintaining your emotional balance and resilience.

Integrating emotional intelligence and resilience into your daily life is a transformative process. It involves a continuous practice of being aware of and managing your emotions, approaching life's challenges with a resilient mindset, and finding a balance between understanding yourself and empathizing with others. Over time, these practices not only enhance your ability to navigate your emotional world but also empower you to face life's ups and downs with a sense of optimism and strength.

The development of emotional intelligence and resilience is a journey of personal growth, especially valuable after experiencing challenging relationships. These skills are not just about coping with what life throws at you; they are about thriving, growing, and finding a deeper sense of fulfillment in your interactions with the world.

Establishing and Attaining Personal Goals

Setting and achieving personal goals is a dynamic process that aligns with your values and desires. The key is to set goals that are not only ambitious but also realistic and attainable. Start by reflecting on what matters most to you. What aspects of your life do you want to improve or change? These could range from personal well-being and career advancement to nurturing relationships or pursuing hobbies. Once you have a clear idea of what you want to achieve, break these goals down into smaller, manageable steps. This approach makes the goals less daunting and more achievable. For instance, if your goal is to improve your physical health, start with smaller objectives, like incorporating a 30-minute walk into your daily routine or choosing healthier meal options.

Strategies for Achieving Goals:

1. Create a Plan: Outline a clear plan of action for each goal. This plan should include specific steps, timelines, and resources needed. A well-structured plan serves as a roadmap, guiding you toward your goal.

2. Stay Consistent: Consistency is key to achieving goals. Regularly review your progress and stay committed to your plan. Even small, consistent efforts can lead to significant results over time.

3. Adapt and Overcome: Be prepared to adapt your plan if circumstances change. Flexibility is important, as it allows you to navigate unforeseen challenges without losing sight of your goal.

4. Seek Support: Do not hesitate to seek support or guidance. This could be from friends, family, mentors, or professionals.

A support system can provide motivation, advice, and accountability.

5. Celebrate Milestones: Acknowledge and celebrate your progress, no matter how small. Celebrating milestones keeps you motivated and reinforces the positive journey you are on.

6. Maintain Focus and Clarity: Keep your goals clear and focused. Avoid spreading yourself too thin by pursuing too many goals at once. Concentrate on a few key objectives that are most important to you, ensuring that your efforts are directed and effective.

7. Visualize Success: Practice visualization. Imagine achieving your goals and the feelings associated with success. Visualization can be a powerful motivator and can help keep you inspired and focused on your objectives.

8. Learn From Setbacks: View setbacks not as failures but as learning opportunities. Analyze what went wrong and what could be done differently. This approach helps you build resilience and adaptability, which are crucial for long-term success.

9. Time Management: Prioritize your tasks and manage your time effectively. Good time management allows you to work on your goals without neglecting other important aspects of your life.

10. Stay Motivated: Find ways to keep your motivation high. This could be through inspirational reading, listening to motivational speakers, or surrounding yourself with people who encourage and inspire you.

11. Adjust Goals as Needed: Be open to reassessing and adjusting your goals as your life changes. Flexibility is important, as it allows your goals to remain relevant and aligned with your current situation and values.

12. Practice Self-Discipline: Cultivate self-discipline. Staying committed to your goals, even when they are challenging or

when the initial excitement has waned, is essential for achieving them.

13. Mindfulness and Stress Management: Practice mindfulness and stress management techniques. Keeping your stress levels in check and staying present can improve your focus and efficiency in working toward your goals.

14. Seek Feedback: Do not be afraid to ask for feedback. Constructive criticism can provide valuable insights and help you refine your approach to achieving your goals.

15. Stay Healthy: Maintain a healthy lifestyle. Your physical and mental well-being both play a significant role in your ability to stay focused and energized while pursuing your goals.

By incorporating these strategies into your goal-setting and achievement processes, you can enhance your ability to reach your aspirations effectively. Remember, the journey toward your goals is a dynamic one, requiring persistence, adaptability, and a positive mindset.

Embracing Vulnerability as a Source of Strength

In the journey of personal development, particularly after navigating life's challenges, embracing vulnerability emerges as a profound strength. This concept, often misconstrued, is not about exposing oneself to harm but about having the courage to be open, honest, and authentically oneself. It is in this brave act of revealing true feelings, dreams, and fears that one finds a powerful catalyst for growth and connection.

Vulnerability serves as the gateway to deeper, more meaningful relationships. It entails a willingness to share one's inner world, fostering a sense of belonging and understanding that arises only from genuine connections. It involves breaking down walls and constructing bridges, fostering bonds rooted in authenticity and mutual respect.

Transforming vulnerability into empowerment is a journey of recognizing that revealing one's true self is a choice reflective of strength. It enables individuals to live more fully, embracing both the joys and challenges of life without the constraints of pretense. Each instance of choosing vulnerability is an embrace of personal freedom and self-acceptance, stepping into one's authentic power. Furthermore, vulnerability cultivates resilience. It imparts the lesson that facing life's uncertainties is natural and that inner strength exists to overcome them. This resilience is not born out of avoidance but out of confronting and embracing the full spectrum of human experience. It is a realistic, grounded resilience enriched by each unique experience.

In the realm of personal growth, embracing vulnerability entails honesty about strengths and areas for improvement. It involves setting goals that resonate with one's true self and pursuing them with an open heart. It also means being open to seeking help, and understanding that reaching out for support is not a sign of weakness but an indication of strength and wisdom.

Embracing vulnerability is an uplifting journey. Each moment of openness is an opportunity for growth, a chance to learn more about oneself, deepen relationships, and live a more authentic life. Approach these moments with positivity and openness, recognizing that they shape an individual into a more empathic, resilient, and genuine person. In essence, vulnerability is not merely a facet of personal development; it is a cornerstone. It is about celebrating one's true self, forging deep connections, and navigating life's challenges with courage and optimism. Let vulnerability be a guiding force toward a life of authenticity, resilience, and fulfillment, transforming every challenge into an opportunity for growth.

Navigating Life Changes and Embracing New Beginnings

Life unfolds as a dynamic journey, marked by unexpected twists and turns. It is within the tapestry of transitions that we often uncover our greatest strengths and discover avenues for personal growth.

Change, though at times intimidating, is a natural and vital aspect of existence. It acts as the impetus propelling us forward, urging us to evolve and develop. Whether manifested in alterations to our career, relationships, location, or personal aspirations, each change carries the potential to explore uncharted horizons and possibilities. It beckons us to step beyond our comfort zones and unveil aspects of ourselves that may have remained dormant.

Navigating life changes is not just about adapting to new circumstances; it is about embracing them with an open heart and a positive mindset. It is recognizing that every change, no matter how challenging, carries within it the seeds of new opportunities. These opportunities might be for learning, personal development, or forging new connections and experiences that enrich our lives.

One of the most beautiful aspects of embracing change is the fresh perspective it brings. It is an opportunity to see the world through a different lens, to reevaluate what is important to us, and to redefine our paths. This process of reevaluation and adaptation is not just about survival; it is about thriving. It is about finding joy and fulfillment in new beginnings and using them as stepping stones to build the life we desire. Furthermore, change often instills a renewed sense of hope and optimism. It serves as a reminder that life is not stagnant, that our past does not dictate our future, and that boundless possibilities await. With each new beginning, we are given a chance to start afresh, to sow new seeds, and to grow in directions we may never have imagined.

In embracing life's changes and new beginnings, remember to be kind to yourself. Allow yourself the time to adjust, to learn, and to grow. Seek support from friends, family, or professionals if needed, and know that it is okay to feel uncertain or overwhelmed at times. These feelings are part of the journey and are stepping stones to greater understanding and resilience. Life's changes and new beginnings are opportunities dressed in disguise. They are chances to explore, to grow, and to reinvent ourselves. Approach these changes with optimism and an open heart, and let them be the catalysts for a life filled with hope, joy, and endless possibilities. Remember, in the grand adventure of life, every change is a new chapter waiting to be written, filled with potential and promise.

Chapter 16:
Life Beyond Narcissistic Bonds

Embracing a Life of Balance

For empaths, achieving a sense of balance is akin to mastering an art form—a nuanced dance between immersing themselves in the emotions of the world and safeguarding their inner sanctum. This equilibrium is not merely a desirable state; it is crucial for the well-being and contentment of individuals who navigate life with heightened sensitivity.

Empaths experience the world in vivid emotional colors. Each interaction, each moment can be a brushstroke of someone else's feelings on the canvas of their psyche. The beauty of this trait lies in its profound depth of understanding and connection with others. Yet, this same depth can become overwhelming, blurring the lines between the emotions of the self and those of others. The challenge, therefore, lies in finding a middle ground where empathy enriches personal experiences without overshadowing one's emotional health.

The importance of this balance cannot be overstated. Without it, empaths may find themselves drained, lost in a sea of external emotions, struggling to anchor themselves to their own sense of self. On the other hand, when balance is achieved, empaths can harness their gift, using it to connect, heal, and understand, while also enjoying a wellspring of personal peace and stability.

Discovering balance is a profoundly individual journey, differing from one person to another. It involves understanding one's emotional thresholds and recognizing signs of emotional overload. Navigating the emotional landscapes of others without losing sight of one's emotional horizon is key to this process. This equilibrium allows empaths to remain open and receptive to others' feelings while firmly rooted in their emotional ground.

Furthermore, maintaining this balance is an ongoing process—a continuous tuning of one's emotional strings to the symphony of life. It requires a conscious effort to stay connected with one's inner world, acknowledging and honoring personal feelings and needs. Allowing oneself to retreat and rejuvenate when the emotional noise of the world becomes overwhelming is an integral part of this delicate balance.

In essence, the balance between empathy and personal well-being serves as the cornerstone of an empath's journey. It enables them to flourish, embracing their unique way of experiencing the world while safeguarding their emotional health and joy. Like a tree that stands firm and tall yet sways gracefully with the wind, an empath in balance is both deeply rooted and beautifully responsive to the emotional winds of the world.

Empathic Wisdom in Everyday Life

As you navigate through your day, your profound emotional sensitivity is not merely a trait; it serves as a guide. It aids you in maneuvering through interactions with a deep understanding, transforming ordinary moments into chances for meaningful connection. This distinctive perspective acts as your compass in a world where emotions frequently go unexpressed and unnoticed.

Consider how this insight shapes your conversations. Your engagement with others goes beyond a simple exchange of words. Instead, you attune yourself to the emotions underlying those words, discerning subtleties that others might overlook. This ability empowers you to provide a level of support and comprehension that can have a profound impact. It is your way of turning routine exchanges into moments of genuine human connection.

In your professional environment, this intuitive understanding becomes a significant asset. You possess the ability to perceive the emotional atmosphere of your workplace, empathize with colleagues, and navigate intricate interpersonal dynamics. This sensitivity makes you a valuable team member, contributing not only through skills and knowledge but also through emotional intelligence.

In your personal relationships, this intuitive insight deepens your connections. You naturally understand and empathize with your loved ones, often anticipating their needs and emotions. This establishes a robust foundation of trust and mutual understanding, enriching your relationships with depth and sincerity.

However, harnessing this insight also involves knowing when to step back. Recognizing the boundaries between yourself and others is crucial. It is important to encourage those around you to express themselves and find their own solutions. Your role is not always to absorb or solve their emotional challenges, but to offer support and understanding while allowing them space to grow.

Turn this intuitive insight inward as well. Reflect on your emotional responses and experiences. This introspection goes beyond self-analysis; it is about understanding how your emotional experiences connect you to others. It deepens your self-awareness and enhances your ability to navigate life with empathy and understanding.

Your profound emotional sensitivity is a gift, one that enables you to experience the world in a rich and connected way. Embrace this gift, using it to enhance your life and the lives of those around you. Your sensitivity has the power to bring comfort, understanding, and healing, not just to yourself but to the world you inhabit.

Your journey involves deep emotional connections. It is a path that transforms everyday experiences into opportunities for growth, understanding, and meaningful interaction. Embrace this journey with an open heart, and let your intuitive insight illuminate your way.

Expressing Creativity as an Empath

In your life as an empath, the depth of your emotional experiences can sometimes feel overwhelming. Yet, within this depth lies a wellspring of creativity—a channel through which you can express and process the rich tapestry of feelings you encounter. Creative expression, in its many forms, offers you a unique way to navigate your empathic nature, transforming the intensity of your emotions into art that speaks both to you and to others.

Imagine each emotion as a color on a palette, each with its unique hue and texture. Through creative activities, you blend and shape these colors, giving form to what you feel in a way that words alone cannot capture. This process is not just about creating art; it is a form of communication with your inner self, a dialogue that helps you understand and make sense of your emotional landscape.

The beauty of this creative journey is that it is deeply personal and entirely yours. Whether through painting, where strokes and shades on the canvas mirror the emotions within you, or writing, where your words weave intricate emotions into narratives and reflections, or through music, dance, or photography, each medium provides a unique outlet for your emotional expression. The key is to find the form that resonates with your soul, one that feels like an extension of your inner world.

This creative expression is not just a solitary journey; it can also serve as a bridge to others. Sharing your art is a way of sharing your empathic insights, offering a window into the depth of your emotional understanding. It is an invitation to others to connect with you on a profound level, to see the world through your empathic lens. This sharing can be a powerful experience, creating connections and understanding that transcend words.

Moreover, embracing creativity is an act of self-care—a necessary and nurturing practice in your life as an empath. In a world where you often absorb so much from others, your creative space is a sanctuary. It is a place where you can focus on your voice, where you can simply be with your emotions without judgment or the need to resolve them for others. This time is essential for your well-being, allowing you to recharge and maintain your emotional equilibrium.

Your creative expression is a harmonious blend of your empathy and your voice. It is a journey that not only helps you process and understand your emotions but also enriches your life with beauty and depth. As you continue to explore and embrace your creativity, let it be a guiding light in your empathic journey, illuminating your path with color, understanding, and connection.

Building and Nurturing Empathic Networks

As an empath, establishing bonds with others who share your depth of feeling and understanding is not merely comforting; it is a transformative experience. These empathic networks, communities of like-minded individuals, provide you with a space where the richness of your emotional world is not only acknowledged but celebrated. The process of building these networks is a journey of exploration where you seek and connect with individuals who fluently speak the language of empathy.

Discovering these connections often involves exploring various avenues. It might entail joining groups or communities focused on empathy, emotional well-being, and personal growth. These spaces can offer you a sense of belonging and the realization that your experiences as an empath are shared by many. Whether in online forums, local clubs, or support groups, these communities become a reflection of your empathic nature. At times, you may find yourself forging these paths, creating spaces for others to join. Initiating a group or community platform can be a powerful way to bring together like-minded individuals. In creating these spaces, the emphasis lies on cultivating an atmosphere of openness, acceptance, and mutual respect. It is about providing a haven where everyone feels comfortable sharing their experiences and insights.

Within these empathic networks, the relationships you cultivate are rooted in a profound understanding and a shared emotional language. It extends beyond offering support; it involves mutual growth, learning from one another, and strengthening your collective capacity for empathy. These connections allow for a rich exchange of experiences and perspectives, enhancing your understanding of your empathic nature. The impact of these networks transcends personal growth and support; they act as small ecosystems of empathy, radiating understanding and compassion into broader circles. The collective experiences and insights within the network contribute to fostering a more empathic and connected society.

Building and nurturing empathic networks are vital aspects of your life as an empath. These networks provide a space where you can fully engage with your empathic nature in a supportive and understanding environment. They offer a platform for shared growth, a place where you can connect with others on a profound level, and a community where your unique way of experiencing the world is not just understood but valued. As you continue to develop these connections, you enrich not only your own life but also contribute to creating a more empathic world.

Looking Ahead With Hope and Empowerment

At this juncture in your life, armed with a deeper understanding of your empathic nature, gaze into the future with a sense of hope and empowerment. Your journey as an empath extends beyond a personal expedition; it possesses the potential to touch lives and instigate positive change in the world. Your empathic nature is a unique gift, enabling you to connect, understand, and heal in profound and essential ways.

Envision the future as a blank canvas, awaiting your brush to paint it with the vibrant hues of your empathy and understanding. Each stroke you make on this canvas carries the potential to infuse beauty, depth, and significance not only into your own life but also into the lives of those around you. Your profound ability to feel, empathize, and connect constitutes a powerful force for good, capable of bridging divides, mending wounds, and cultivating a more compassionate world.

Approach this future with optimism. The challenges you have confronted and the lessons you have assimilated have endowed you with incredible strength and wisdom. These experiences have refined your empathic abilities, transforming them into instruments for positive change. As you progress, employ these tools to effect change, making a meaningful impact in your community and contributing to a world that values empathy and emotional connection.

Bear in mind that your journey as an empath is not solitary. You are part of a community of kindred spirits, each endowed with their unique empathic gifts. Together, your collective empathy possesses the potential to create ripples of change, inspire others, and foster a culture of understanding and compassion. Your individual journey weaves into this collective movement, adding to the tapestry of empathic transformation.

Cast your gaze toward the future as a realm of possibilities—a future where your empathic nature is not only accepted but celebrated. Imagine a future where the depth of your emotions is acknowledged as a strength, a fount of wisdom and insight. In this future, you, as an empath, play a pivotal role in shaping a more empathic and understanding society. As you propel forward, carry with you a sense of hope and empowerment. Allow these sentiments to guide you along your path, utilizing your empathic nature to illuminate shadowy corners, provide solace in times of pain, and foster understanding in the face of conflict. Your journey as an empath stands as a powerful testament to humanity's capacity for empathy, connection, and positive change.

Continue on your path with the understanding that your empathic nature is a gift to the world. It possesses the power to transform, heal, and pave the way for a brighter future. Embrace this journey with an open heart and an optimistic spirit, letting your empathy be the guiding light that leads you forward.

A Note of Gratitude and Invitation for Your Thoughts

Dear Reader,

As we come to the end of our journey together, I hope that the insights and strategies shared have been both enlightening and empowering. Understanding and healing from the complexities of relationships is a challenging yet rewarding path.

Your experiences and insights are invaluable. By sharing your genuine and honest review on Amazon, you offer a guiding light to others who are navigating similar challenges. Your perspective can be a source of hope and strength to many.

As an independent author, your feedback is crucial. It not only supports the growth and reach of my work but also helps others discover resources that could be pivotal in their healing journey.

I invite you to take a moment to share your thoughts about the book on Amazon. Whether it is about how the content resonated with you, what you learned, or its impact on your perspective, your honest review is deeply appreciated.

Thank you for your time, your trust, and for being a part of this important conversation. I eagerly look forward to reading your reflections.

Warm regards,

Rachel

Scan to leave a review on
Amazon if you live in the US

Scan to leave a review on
Amazon if you live in the UK

Scan to leave a review on
Amazon if you live in Canada

Scan to leave a review on
Amazon if you live in Australia

About the Author

R achel West is a compassionate guide and mentor, dedicated to helping individuals navigate the complexities of emotional and relational dynamics. With a deep understanding of the intricacies of empathic personalities and the challenges posed by narcissistic relationships, Rachel has devoted her career to supporting those seeking to heal from toxic relationships and thrive in their personal growth. Her journey into the realm of relationship dynamics and self-healing began with her own experiences and observations. Rachel's keen interest in human behavior and emotional wellness led her to immerse herself in extensive research and exploration of various healing modalities. She has a unique ability to blend intuitive understanding with practical strategies, creating a holistic approach to healing and empowerment.

Rachel's work is characterized by a profound empathy and a genuine desire to assist others in recognizing their worth and potential. She believes in the power of self-awareness and self-care as key components in breaking free from negative cycles and building healthier, more fulfilling relationships. Her approach is not just about overcoming challenges but also about embracing one's strengths and cultivating a life of balance and joy. Beyond her professional endeavors, Rachel is an avid reader and a lifelong learner, constantly seeking new insights and perspectives. She finds solace and inspiration in nature, often spending her free time in the tranquility of the outdoors, where she reconnects with herself and the world around her. Rachel also enjoys creative writing, seeing it as a therapeutic tool for expression and self-discovery.

Rachel's commitment to her work stems from a deep-seated belief in the resilience of the human spirit and the transformative power of understanding and compassion. Through her guidance, many have found the courage to face their fears, embrace their true selves, and embark on a journey toward healing and fulfillment. Her empathic nature and insightful guidance make her a trusted ally in the journey toward emotional well-being and personal growth.

Made in the USA
Las Vegas, NV
02 August 2024

93281026R00089